THE SHADOW PRESIDENT

THE
SHADOW
PRESIDENT

TED KENNEDY IN OPPOSITION

BURTON HERSH

STEERFORTH PRESS

SOUTH ROYALTON, VERMONT

Library of Congress Cataloging-in-Publication Data
Hersh, Burton.
The shadow president : Ted Kennedy in opposition / Burton Hersh.
        p.   cm.
Includes index.
ISBN 1-883642-30-2 (alk. paper)
1. Kennedy, Edward Moore, 1932–   . 2. Legislators — United States —
Biography.   3. United States. Congress. Senate — Biography.   4. United
States — Politics and government — 1945–1989.   5. United States —
Politics and government — 1989–   6. Liberalism — United States —
History — 20th century. I. Title.
E840.8.K35H43   1997
973.92 '092 — dc21
        [B]   97-3109
            CIP

Credits for photo insert: Page 1, Kennedy Library. Page 2, top, AP; bottom, Courtesy Robert Shrum. Page 3, top, Kennedy Library; bottom, Courtesy Office of Senator Edward Kennedy. Page 4, AP. Page 5, Kennedy Library. Page 6, top, Kennedy Library; bottom, AP. Page 7, Kennedy Library. Page 8, top, AP; bottom, Kennedy Library.

Manufactured in the United States of America

FIRST EDITION

"His brothers were great human beings, but they
couldn't carry his shoes as a legislator."
Senator Orrin Hatch, Conservative Republican, Utah, 1994

"When he [Edward Kennedy] finally lifted the
curse from himself that Kennedys had to be president,
he truly became a legislator."
*Senator Alan Simpson, Conservative Republican,
Wyoming, 1994*

"Below the belt all men are brothers."
*Henry Miller,
An Open Letter to Surrealists Everywhere*

For John Hiatt

A great friend, and a survivor

FOREWORD

Twenty-seven years ago, after quite a frank exchange one morning in his Boston residence at Charles River Square, Edward Kennedy hauled himself out of his chair to accompany me to the street. Just off the vestibule he pulled up to direct my attention to a framed letter by Daniel Webster, which he took time enough to read aloud. Webster was a hero of Kennedy's, an opinionated yet in the end incorruptible advocate for Massachusetts in both the U.S. House of Representatives and the U.S. Senate for thirty-seven years, punctuated by stretches as Secretary of State as well as an abortive campaign as Whig candidate for U.S. president.

I had been sounding Kennedy out in the midst of his 1970 campaign for the Senate, which found him grinding through the days destabilized by the Chappaquiddick disaster the year before. Many of his colleagues had distanced themselves, yet, within the Senate itself, Kennedy was emerging more plainly every session as a spearpoint of the anti-war Left, an increasingly telling critic of the Nixon administration's evasive and costly maneuvering to mask its embroilment in Vietnam. The lunatic Right simmered; Kennedy was openly worried, as he would confess to a friend, that he was about to "get my ass blown off."

Tough as things got at times, what impressed me even in those days was Kennedy's extraordinary detachment, the way he was able to keep his predicament in context. I had been working since 1967 on a full-length biography — ultimately, *The Education of Edward Kennedy,* which would be published in 1972 — and hard as I found it much of the time to draw Kennedy out, to get him to speculate about the sources of his own behavior, I suspect he gave himself away to a certain extent with his admiration for Webster. Daniel Webster had staying power. He had an impact on the civilization of his time. An unremitting old toper in private life, his preoccupation was not in the end with his reputation or his personal fortune but rather the prospects of the divided Republic. No setback could scuttle him. He defined an age.

Bludgeoned incessantly by controversy, Webster could maintain himself. So could Edward Kennedy. Kennedy had taken punishment, much of it self-inflicted. Something of an afterthought among the nine children of frequently absentee parents, Kennedy conditioned his reflexes while bouncing in and out of school after school, winding up at Harvard, which threw him out for a couple of years for cheating on his Spanish exam. When Kennedy first promoted the idea of running in 1962, his primary opponent Eddie McCormack railed out in debate that if he were not the president's brother "your candidacy would be a joke." Advisors to John Kennedy tended to agree; one of them, Harvard Law professor Mark deWolfe Howe, termed Teddy's efforts "reckless, childishly irresponsible." Insiders around Cambridge anticipated that this lightweight pretender to JFK's old Senate seat would hold it as long as his brother occupied the White House.

The next year John Kennedy died in Dallas. In 1964 the Aero Commander in which Ted Kennedy was flying up for the Democratic convention in Springfield plummeted into an apple orchard in the fog. Kennedy spent that autumn trussed into a Stryker frame, every vertebra fractured. In January of 1965 he reappeared in the Senate, noticeably dragging one leg and reconciled to a lifetime of chronic pain.

In 1968 the irreplaceable Bobby was shot to death in the Hotel Ambassador's kitchen in Los Angeles. A year later Edward Kennedy's battered Oldsmobile skidded off the bridge at Chappaquiddick. He survived the scandal in Massachusetts, but allies and columnists agreed that he was finished as a national phenomenon.

I wondered even then what continued to sustain him. Kennedy's marriage was tortured, his children visibly upset and frightened. I thought he fed on myth too much of the time. "This place is so much a part of all the Kennedys," he himself had scrawled across the margin of a limited-edition silk-screen of the family compound at Hyannis Port he sent me in 1970. He'd painted the original, a melange of peaks and gables as seen from the churning rockbound ocean.

When I started tracking Kennedy, on assignment from *Esquire* in 1967, Ted continued to define himself as Robert Kennedy's kid brother. Sharper, more restless, a lot less collegial — Bobby and his ambitions remained preeminent, always. The kind of press Ted attracted had to be adjusted at all times with an eye to Bobby's prospects. All three Kennedy brothers treated print journalism like so much electoral technology — something to be exploited, controlled, manipulated to their requirements.

Neither the embellishment of ego nor the validation of history had much to do with whatever got cooperation.

I understood this early, so I was not surprised to discover that, while Kennedy as an acquaintance has always seemed well-disposed, the access I've gotten as a journalist has varied according to his circumstances at the time we talked. When things are upbeat, and he's being universally lionized, he's difficult to corner. My way of nosing into relief the fault lines and rough spots of Kennedy's character understandably makes him skittish. I've never let anybody I've written about review manuscript prior to publication, and that caused something of a problem in 1972. Undoubtedly touchiest of all, a number of the loyalists he depends on have turned into friends of mine. Yet I've been dedicated over the years, and emphasized his compounding political contributions. And so when everything is collapsing, Kennedy tends to open up his schedule for me.

One of Kennedy's talents — unique among the politicians I've dealt with — is his capacity to step back even during the worst of disasters and contemplate the entire scene, particularly his own ineptitude, with mordant appreciation. This comes through again and again in correspondence we've had. Pre-publication magazine excerpts from *The Education of Edward Kennedy,* for example, had highlighted his hectic and increasingly alcoholic behavior the spring leading into the Chappaquiddick episode. Kennedy's press aide, Dick Drayne, had run me down by telephone in Vail after one piece appeared to chew my head off personally. The staff was roiled up, yet again.

Kennedy himself stayed out of it. Then, once the biography was published, he wrote me in another connection, and added toward the end of the note that he hadn't "had the chance to read your book from one end to the other, but have glanced at some of the chapters, especially the references to Jack Crimmins." Crimmins served as Kennedy's driver around Boston at that time. It was to spare this choleric street Irishman the chore of chauffeuring the senator and Mary Jo Kopechne to the ferry landing at Chappaquiddick that Kennedy had taken the fateful wheel himself.

I'd quoted Crimmins's choicer observations here and there in *The Education,* such as his aside one day while we were passing MIT that faculty in there were "softer than a sneaker full of puppy shit." I'd heard that Crimmins got quite worked up. Kennedy knew about that, and now he intended to tweak me in passing as well as reestablish his own stance above the flack of publicity. He presumed we both would recognize a professional relationship.

Even before Bobby died, Ted Kennedy was losing himself in the contemplation of the Senate. He'd started to explore power, its usages, its seductiveness. Involvement stimulated the adrenals; effort annealed the emotions. Like alcohol or revelry, work could protect you from your thoughts. Unlike his two brothers, who in the end had taken the government by storm, Edward Kennedy now grasped that it was possible to build influence out in a place like the Senate in such a way that in the end one became impregnable. One became a power center, a kind of counterpart to the presidency itself.

This could take decades, of course, but Kennedy was comfortable with decades. And more than that, he had the temperament for such a grind. He is the only man in public life I know who routinely refers to himself as a "politician," with all the cigar smoke and obnoxious deal-making a term like that has come to exude. The Senate is a small world, ninety-nine colleagues, and generation by generation Kennedy has expended his charm on virtually every one. He can be irascible sometimes, with a weakness for demagoguing issues, but there is nobody else out there to match Kennedy's talent for sizing people up and factoring in the particulars.

Along with tactical skill, Kennedy had taken on gravity enough to occupy his convictions. He's never been much put off at being called a liberal, and battled for three decades to prevent the entire society from becoming a trough for the interests. Yet at the same time Kennedy saw right away that on a day-to-day basis even a James Eastland or a Strom Thurmond or a Dan Quayle wasn't ideologically monolithic, there would be sentiments or points of honor or even a glimmer of patriotism through which to lure them into camp as opportunity presented. It's been Kennedy's aptitude for coalition-building which convulsed successive White House staffs. Democratic and Republican presidents alike have found the success of their administrations was coming to depend on Edward Kennedy's willingness to bring his friends along. Even when he lost, he altered the presumptions of the debate and opened the way for victories later on.

Taking on so many assignments, across such an unequaled spectrum, Kennedy continued to overlap the constituencies which looked to him for expertise and support. They ran in time from the traditional voiceless minorities and labor union functionaries to biomedical programmers and flight controllers and C.E.O.s in emerging technologies and big-city prosecuting attorneys and movie stars and immigrants (documented and otherwise) and retired senior military and Archbishop Desmond Tutu and New Bedford fishermen just in from the Grand Banks. Endlessly curious, irresistibly involved, Edward Kennedy would peruse our life down to the finest human print.

In 1972 I imagined I'd told Kennedy's story. It had barely opened. Even what I've added here may amount to no more than an impressionistic second installment. Battered as we find ourselves by politics these days, that may be just as well.

Burton Hersh
Bradford, New Hampshire
1997

I

It was the worst of times, again. It required the entire summer of 1991 to drag him to the podium, throughout which the pounding by the media only seemed to scale up in ferocity, and chits were expended to quash a censure hearing, and he himself sat stony and ineffectual above the Clarence Thomas proceedings, and even his ex-wife Joan broke back into the headlines by losing her Massachusetts driver's license after one too many citations for rolling around fried. "I am painfully aware that the criticism directed at me in recent months involves far more than honest disagreement with my positions," he intoned before a hand-picked audience at the Kennedy School that October, "or the usual criticism from the far right. I recognize my own shortcomings — the faults in the conduct of my private life. I realize that I alone am responsible for them, and I alone must confront them."

It was as if, en tableau, hovering over the fifty-nine-year-old Edward Kennedy, just beyond the television lights, images of the Easter recess floated. Kennedy at the Au Bar, slumped above a table in the corner with his restive son Patrick and his nephew Willy Smith at three in the morning Easter Sunday, absorbing whiskey and holding court to a procession of divorcées and barflies half his age. Returned to the Palm Beach mansion, drifting in his nightshirt like an enormous moth across the gloom toward Patrick and one of the women they had enticed back to La Guerida, then hanging there above the pair in the shadowy ground-floor sitting room until Patrick's partner — unable later to remember precisely whether she had anything on at the time — felt so "weirded out" that she had given it up and fled. Resting in his bedroom, finally, and purportedly unable to hear or respond to the terrified screams for help Patricia Bowman, Willy Smith's acquisition, claimed she had sounded all across the lawns from the gritty beach where Smith was alleged to be assaulting her by then, horsing off her panties and grinding up flotsam and debris into her underparts in his determination to *get-this-over-with. . . .*

Images of America's nobility. News of the incident had spread within hours, with never any hope it could be contained in the tabloids or burned out as incidental news, buried in the mainstream press. Like anything that related to Edward Kennedy, as the nineties opened, the atmosphere was richly overloaded. A decade of mid-life bachelordom had not been generous to Kennedy, he acted it and looked it, and well before Willy Smith's adventure brought down the firestorm, even the nonpartisan "life-style" magazines were conditioning a receptive public.

In February of 1990, more than a year ahead of the Palm Beach incident, Michael Kelly took aim and epitomized his subject in GQ as a "Senator Bedfellow figure, an aging Irish boyo clutching a bottle and diddling a blonde." Kelly would remain particularly unsparing wherever it came to Kennedy's appearance: "Up close, the face is a shock. The skin has gone from red roses to gin blossoms. The tracery of burst capillaries shines faintly through the scaly scarlet patches that cover the bloated, mottled cheeks." In no hurry, Kelly works his way down the topography of Kennedy's face — the bulbous nose, the corrugated forehead, the Chiclet teeth. "The eyes have yellowed too, and they are so bloodshot, it looks as if he's been weeping."

At fifty-seven, Kennedy struck Kelly as primarily a "'husk,' dried up and hollowed out," uncertain in his gait, fluttery, living out a perpetual morning after, staggering through his "autumn years." Was anyone genuinely surprised the night the Palm Beach incident torched whatever was left of Ted Kennedy's reputation?

Kennedy had been left for dead before, of course. Once footage from the 1991 Easter weekend started to unroll, no one in the media could help but summon up details from another vacation weekend, in July almost twenty-two years earlier, when Edward Kennedy's Oldsmobile had skidded off the Dike Bridge at Chappaquiddick Island. Kennedy had somehow escaped; Mary Jo Kopechne drowned.

Then too the press had literally laid siege, reporters by the hundreds, standing around in clumps outside the hedges of the sprawling estate of Joseph P. Kennedy in Hyannis Port. Frustrated with the lack of news, exchanging theories, until the toxicity of the rumors by the end of the week seemed all but guaranteed to extinguish the surviving Kennedy son.

It all seemed hallucinated to me, even at the time. One year before that, a matter of months after Bobby was gunned down, Edward Kennedy had very nearly found himself conscripted as the Democratic candidate for president in Chicago. The votes, evidently, were there. In place of the tall, halting figure in the neck brace with the buffaloed look on his handsome stricken face being conducted in and out of cars headed for preliminary proceedings in the Edgartown courtroom, this might by then have been a thirty-seven-year-old American president. Political fortunes come about on a dime in this country, but this was stunning.

Stunning to me especially. I was that summer of 1969 perhaps two years into a full-scale biography of Edward Kennedy. When I had started, Senator Robert Kennedy alone incarnated the family's presidential ambitions. Then for a year after Bobby's assassination, Edward Kennedy had seemed — especially from afar — to be maturing by the month to fill the role, legatee to the fallen standard. Then came the Chappaquiddick incident, followed by the quickly spreading presumption that Edward Kennedy was finished.

That made sense. What reporters generally missed — what I missed sometimes over the course of the stomach-churning cycles of Kennedy's career — was that his importance did not depend, in the last analysis, on his momentary popularity with the press, or the accidents of his episodic personal life, or his undeniable drinking, or even repute among the colleagues. Kennedy's career was buoyed up early and late by the extraordinary depth and commitment of his political calling, his sense of what he has been charged to effectuate in the public arena. Ordinary people picked that up, they responded to that.

Just as her religious intensity sustained Rose Kennedy through the violent and untimely deaths of four of her children and the retardation of a fifth, so Edward Kennedy's integrity of political mission would remain so immediate to him, so solid, that in the end no tragedy, no scandal has yet been able to drag him down or lure him permanently off course. The people

Kennedy depends on, those closest to him, are sure at least of the sincerity of his dedication to the vulnerable, the otherwise unprotected millions. Neither Jack nor Bobby even was ever quite able to ground a political identity in bedrock this unshakable. The decades of sporadic adolescent shenanigans that would have — in fact, have always — plowed under the reputation and crippled the performance of a lesser politician leave Kennedy amazingly viable. Commitment keeps coming through — Ted Kennedy is larger than his appetites.

This had a lot to do, I determined over time, with his intense if multilayered involvement with his family. Not merely the individuals, but more than that the ethos, the *legend* of who the Kennedys were and what they were supposed to be. For Jack and Bobby — and certainly for the manipulative Ambassador Joe — the glorification of the Kennedys had been by way of public relations hype, something of a tool, a highly saleable myth they merchandised into power and votes. For Ted, ultimately, Camelot opened around him, a kind of glorious if intimidating confinement. It remained a distillation of painfully noble purposes, a vision so demanding that for years his inability to flesh out its possibilities had almost a stunting effect on Ted, it set back the evolution of his personality by decades.

I'd been repeatedly struck during the first years of my exchanges with Kennedy by how often and reflexively he referred to his brothers — what they had thought about this issue or that, how what he was proposing that season advanced the concerns of the late president or the fallen senator. For years this came over as artificial to me — an attempt to legitimize himself in the context of their efforts. I suspected at times that even Kennedy's weakness — the random, hectic tomcatting, his propensity for noisy strident moralizing from the podium — amounted to a kind of homage to the pair who left their big, clownish kid brother behind. Acting all this out had a way of telling on Kennedy. Both Chappaquiddick and the Palm Beach incident came out of too many months of mourning for a family member, too extended an awareness of what was lost once and for all.

He was often reminded of his unworthiness. The day Ted finally delivered his maiden speech on the Senate floor, Senator Philip Hart happened to stop by Attorney General Robert Kennedy's office, where he congratulated Bobby on Ted's eloquent presentation. "Teddy gave a good speech?" Bobby reportedly snapped. "I suppose it's possible. Who do you imagine wrote it for him?"

With somebody of less devotion, resentment might have surfaced. Kennedy himself soldiered on, preoccupied with who his family had been, what they had done for him. Soon after the Chappadquiddick episode in the fall of 1969, once Kennedy was back in the Senate, I went to sound him out in the ornate recesses of the Whip's chambers. We dealt with legislation at hand, his health, finally — I proceeded very tentatively here — questions that still needed answering about the accident itself. On that subject he responded in a measured way, gravely, the sadness coming through although he appeared relatively self-possessed. Then (I was preparing to leave) I offered my condolences on the death of his father. Kennedy looked at me; his voice broke; tears sprang into his eyes and started down his cheeks. He still stood prepared to deal with his own troubles, but even the mention of the old buccaneer wobbling paralyzed in his wheelchair stirred too much, it left Kennedy helpless.

The scandal over Chappaquiddick had erupted at a time when Kennedy was facing enough without the inquest at Edgartown. His activism on the Justice committee left him the ringleader of the bloody but successful efforts to block Richard Nixon's successive Supreme Court appointments of Clement Haynsworth and George Harold Carswell, as well as the lead strategist pushing through the extension of the Voting Rights Act. He ground away steadily to exclude the long-standing professional and academic exemptions from the draft lottery, a footnote of historic importance since it would expose the sons of the middle classes to conscription and pressure the Nixon administration into serious negotiations to end the war in Vietnam.

Even Chappaquiddick wasn't enough to convince the White House that Ted was down. "This is quite a day on another front too!" Richard Nixon exulted as the news from Edgartown blanked out the moon landing. "It'll be hard to hush this one up." Nixon's staff investigator John Caulfield quickly dispatched a heavy-duty off-the-books operative, Anthony Ulasewicz, to prowl Martha's Vineyard, and months later the two set up a love nest in Manhattan in a fruitless attempt to ensnare one of the "boiler room girls" who attended the fateful cookout. The following winter Caulfield personally tailed Kennedy throughout a stopover in Hawaii, in hopes of catching him out in a compromised situation. By then Kennedy's sapping tactics in opposition to the war were again bleeding the Nixon administration.

Kennedy felt pressure building. Warhorses among the Democrats remained steamed at Kennedy for ducking away from the nomination in 1968, convinced that he might have retained the White House and spared them years of frustration and powerlessness. He hadn't been ready, Ted kept attempting to explain to anyone who would listen. It wasn't that easy. "Do you know what it's like to have your wife frightened all the time?" He asked one reporter after several drinks. "I'm not afraid to die, I'm too young to die."

It really took all he had to push through the 1970 campaign in Massachusetts, greeting commuters outside subway landings while rounds of testimony stemming from the protracted inquest into the death of Mary Jo Kopechne landed across his campaign like artillery fire. The press remained merciless. "You see this?" Kennedy had demanded, presenting me with that morning's tabloid photo of himself trailed by a perky Italian socialite at Charles de Gaulle's funeral. I had stopped by Kennedy's house on Charles River Square in Boston to pose a few belated questions of my own regarding the accident. "I not only wasn't involved with this woman," Kennedy had exploded. "So far as I know I never clapped eyes on her before or since." In time, with investigation, it developed that Charles Colson at the White House had circulated the photo in a broadscale effort to discredit the recovering senator.

With two brothers shot, it seemed so inescapable at the time that there was some nut out there, up for the hat trick. Kennedy felt that, every conscious minute. I remember in March of 1970 marching with the senator's party in the St. Patrick's Day parade through downtown Lawrence. It was a windy day, raw, the sky all scudding clouds, the streets themselves jammed with kids in ST. MONICA'S warm-up jackets and marchers in morning coats with high green cardboard leprechauns' hats. Halfway through the course some wag set off a cannon cracker; Kennedy's smile froze immediately, I saw his legs buckle and his entire body flinch as he fought the impulse to flatten himself against the asphalt. I remember how ashen he went, how clouded his eyes looked until he recovered himself.

Yet within a few hours he was again marching, this time in South Boston. "This is mission impossible," one of his security handlers muttered as we attempted to press along the close streets, a mob for several miles overflowing against the ropes, cheering, heckling. Joan Kennedy was too terrified to speak.

What police there were attempted to peruse the upper windows of street after street of three-deckers in hopes of spotting the glint of a rifle barrel in time. Halfway through the march a heavyset woman lurched free of the crowd and grabbed Kennedy from the back, hooking up her mammoth doughy forearm and trapping Kennedy around the neck. Somebody in the party immediately fell on her and pried her off; Kennedy gasped for breath, his back in spasm.

"Why'dja do that?" the big woman roared. "Hey, whataya, secret soivuce?"

The parade moved ahead. "Even more than Jack or Bobby, Teddy has an amazing ability to sustain himself," a reporter who'd followed all three around remarked at the time. Unlike his short-fused brothers, Ted had a way of slipping even the most determined assault, of avoiding straightforward personality clashes. "One time with Jack in 1960, there was a newspaper editor in Madison who was giving them fits all through the Wisconsin primary," the reporter recalled. "Jack felt he had to confront this guy and demand at least a semblance of fairness. They talked a while, and Jack wasn't getting anywhere, and finally he said, 'Well, write what you want, you vicious anti-Catholic sonofabitch.'

"And the publisher said, 'Yeah, well, up your ass.'

"It happened that Jackie was there, so she looked up and smiled, and said: 'Well, goodby, Mr. McMillan. It certainly was nice to see you again.'

"My point being, Teddy would have handled it with a little more finesse. On the *professional* level, Ted never forgets that tomorrow will undoubtedly arrive. Privately, of course, he's still a player-arounder in almost a childish sense. He drives too fast, and if he's got some girl he likes he'll show her off to people — you know, laugh, giggle, splash around in the pool. Like a little boy, somebody to fool around with."

Those were the days when politicians had a private life, left out of news columns by unwritten journalist agreement. Kennedy liked women, everybody acknowledged that, not least the heir apparent. This was a feature his friends ascribed to natural warmth, stimulated by the availability of girls. It was an aspect of politics, lagniappe, a sort of droit de seigneur that went with ownership of the electorate. Just as a medieval nobleman might drop off his horse at the sight of some lively peasant girl's well turned haunch among the harvest sheaves, and refresh his loins beneath a noonday sun, so Kennedy had few inhibitions about declaring his interests, then promptly following up. No coercion was involved, nor even much seduction given the customary tight scheduling. He'd been like that at least since adolescence.

All through the sixties in Washington everybody heard the stories. Mid-level State Department officers from New Delhi to Panama City came back with tales of Teddy on senatorial junkets, rousting some poor attaché out of bed at two in the morning to lead him on a crawl among the livelier bordellos. Out West to address a convention, according to another story, the senator picked up a showgirl in Las Vegas toward the end of the evening and settled down afterward in the bedroom of a suite. A local deputy sheriff stood guard outside all night; early the next morning — Kennedy had a plane to catch — the nervous lawman knocked on the bedroom door, waited, then eased inside and tapped the tangle of flesh beneath the sheet on an exposed shoulder. Kennedy reportedly came to, rolled naked and muzzy out onto his feet, and hit the deputy so hard he dislocated his jaw.

A display like that was noteworthy, but rare. Kennedy appreciated fun, he needed to break loose from time to time to shake off the endless overscheduled days in the Senate, the exertion of patience as one hour droned into the next. Dedication was the game; Kennedy played it. "Bobby never really wanted any committee chairmanships, or subcommittee chairmanships," Frank Mankiewicz once observed. For him the Senate remained a way station. Ted aspired to power there, craved responsibility, and almost always took and made the most of whatever he could get and endured with unflagging good humor the endless extra work.

As early as his committee counsel days for Joe McCarthy, Bobby had had a way of boring in on witnesses, rattling loose their inlays. Ted at his most self-righteous and scathing kept open the possibility of redemption. Typical was a grilling I heard him subject an official to at Logan Airport in Boston in 1970 vis-à-vis the facility's antiquated air control system.

After much close questioning, the official ventured hopefully that he would "say the system was safe part of the time."

"What part of the time?" Kennedy wanted to know. "Is it going to be safe when I fly back to Washington tomorrow?"

"Well," the official proposed, "give me your flight number."

Kennedy couldn't help grinning. Bobby might have blown up.

Ted nourished himself on casual exchanges. At Harvard just afterward, at a Winthrop House Forum convened by spokesmen for what was then labeled the Silent Majority, a humorless young student challenged Kennedy as to "whether it might not be possible to produce a Democratic Spiro Agnew."

Kennedy examined her, a warm light emerging in his hooded eyes. "I certainly hope not," he responded after a moment.

2

In fact Kennedy beat the Republican Sy Spaulding fairly easily in 1970, which gave him six more years in which to prove himself, again. It seemed that Ted was always getting driven back, freshly obliged to redeem himself, a Sisyphus for our times.

It did not help to lose his post as Assistant Majority Leader — Whip — to Robert Byrd in 1971. However Snopesian and obsequious, Byrd brought a West Virginian's aptitude for unadvertised favor-trading to what was still in many ways pretty largely a Southerners' club. Even liberals found Kennedy preoccupied, high-handed on occasion, and uninterested in performing the innumerable petty favors on which the functioning of the Senate depends. Majority Leader Mike Mansfield didn't appear to care who won. It seemed to Kennedy that he had the votes, but there were last minute switches and promises never kept.

It plainly hurt Kennedy to surrender his prospects for the leadership to a one-time Kleagle of the Ku Klux Klan. "As your letter suggests," Kennedy wrote me at the time, with typical off-angle humor, "my political fortunes are tied to your book. Every time you think you have finished a manuscript, I can think of a way to send you back to the typewriter for another chapter or two. One of us had better put a stop to it, or you won't have any book, and I won't have any future."

Getting dumped as Whip amounted to the first true political cataclysm Kennedy had ever sustained. He was to react in a way that should have been predictable, Kennedyesque. Old Joe had created an ethos that emphasized that they were unwanted by established society, outsiders, and so would have to depend on nobody, become powers unto themselves. After 1971 Ted Kennedy would concentrate on spreading himself as widely as possible among as many important committees as he could entice into taking him, exerting influence through position and parliamentary mastery independent of the Democratic Party apparatus. He developed a private clientele of outside experts and advisors. He was to preside over a steadily increasing congeries of staffs, a swelling political presence that ultimately cast its shadow across the White House and the Congress itself. He would not again find himself beholden to the liberals, or hesitate to build his alliances where opportunity offered itself, across the entire ideological spectrum. All this would demand a prodigious amount of work. But Kennedy was always a prodigious worker.

Between the open political vendettas brought on by the sputtering war in Vietnam and mass disillusion with politics in the wake of Watergate, little in the way of idealism survived into the Nixon-dominated seventies. Remedial impulses in both parties gave way under Republican administrations to efforts to placate the well-heeled political action committees as campaigns turned increasingly expensive in the age of television. By then Kennedy's long-term agenda was largely in place — tax equity, fairer antitrust implementation, revamping health insurance — and it didn't move very much from year to year. He craved legislative breakthroughs. A bill to deregulate the airlines worked out, and reminded Kennedy how much easier lawmaking became once he and business were moving in the same direction.

Another promising battlefield for bipartisan success was law enforcement. Early in the seventies Kennedy joined with John McClellan in attempting to turn the Brown Commission's recommendations into a remodeled federal criminal code. To work this up Kennedy hired, in 1975, an owlish former assistant U.S. attorney for the Southern District of New York, still seething over abuses of the federal court system by the criminal community. "When I came down here to work for Kennedy," Ken Feinberg remembered, "I told him: I'm a liberal and I'm in favor of housing and all that but as for crime, Senator — crime can't wait!" Kennedy agreed. "I think he found that he'd always been uncomfortable with his stance on criminal justice," Feinberg concluded. "Jim Flug and those people set the senator back on this stuff. Since when have the Kennedys been so permissive in the civil liberties field? Besides" — Feinberg hesitated — "there was a tremendous vacuum opening politically on the right. Hruska was retiring, McClellan was retiring . . . ."

The initial draft, S-1, caught birdshot from so many academic blinds its sponsors pulled back. The successor bill, S-1437, aroused libertarians like Vern Countryman of Harvard Law because of stringency of sentencing, the abolition of parole, and the effort to introduce into the legislation a vague, new category of trespass Countryman called "inchoate crimes," largely conspiratorial intention. Countryman, like the American Civil Liberties Union, felt this was likely to place "outrageously severe limitations" on individual rights to assemble, organize, obtain governmental information, disobey public servants.

Kennedy rolled it through, 72-15, with support that stretched from Gaylord Nelson to Sam Hayakawa. It failed of approval in the House of Representatives, unlike Kennedy's equally controversial reform of federal wiretapping procedures, which now required warrants from a judge but permitted the invasion of conversations which "may" be "harmful to the United States" or against the law. Kennedy pushed through LEAA grants to local police departments.

By 1978 Kennedy's disquiet with Jimmy Carter was mounting; pressure started building overnight across the Democratic Party for Kennedy to bump Carter out in 1980. Kennedy's constituency shifted decisively. The point really wasn't to please the colleagues at that point, there were the black leaders and the labor leaders and all those hairsplitting civil libertarians in the universities a winning Democrat needed. The criminal code's third version, S-1722, emerged half as thick as either of its predecessors, the federal jurisdiction narrowed instead of widened, with lots of excisions in areas that bothered Professor Countryman. "The ACLU performed a valuable service to that legislation," Feinberg's replacement as legislative assistant, Carey Parker, observed. "They flagged ten or fifteen issues they cared about. We left them out."

By spring of 1979 Kennedy's initial flirtation with the troll-ridden right had run its course; Kennedy brother-in-law and campaign strategist Steve Smith was reportedly telephoning his people around the country advising them to preserve their options. Kennedy returned to orthodoxy. This was the spokesman for the "underrepresented," Kennedy of the liberals, chair of the Justice Committee, grizzling at the temples with two fingers curled to mask the susceptible mouth as a lifetime of subcommittee proceedings rolled on beneath those flattering lights. Inspired staff appointments came and went — including Harvard Law School professor Stephen Breyer to work on deregulation, the bright-eyed and enterprising NAACP activist Ron Brown, who opened up new possibilities for Kennedy around DC after dark.

Immovable on the entitlement side, Kennedy had continued throughout the previous decade to find political courage enough to defend forced bussing in Boston, support the ERA, countenance abortion on demand, close down the war in Vietnam, push through the first formal investigation of the burglary at the Watergate, then promote Archibald Cox as special Watergate prosecutor, in the spirit of a prankster insinuating a mastiff into a tank of alley cats.

Openly attacking Jimmy Carter released long-pent energies. "The staff now feels that Kennedy is riding the crest of a wave, that he is immune," said one employee after things got interesting. Office life, as ever, was rough and tumble.

"There is tremendous internal staff competition," remarked one member. "He promotes internal intrigue, he relishes playing one of us off against another to get the most good work out of us. If something goes wrong he'll say, 'Jesus, what's wrong, why haven't you straightened that goddamned thing out?' We do it because the rewards, the recognition, are tremendous." Others around the Hill tended to regard Kennedy's people as bright, but abrasive and pushy. "Kennedy would say, 'Good, that's the only way to get anything done around this fucking place,'" observed one of them. Kennedy himself functioned, now that his staff was largely a generation younger than himself, with a hardy paternalism — a demanding father, much like his own, also well worth listening to. "He'll look at anything, but when it comes to the legislative realities, he'll decide," an aide noted. "He likes to work at home with key people at night. No phone. That's where he educates us."

His administrative aide at that point, the volatile Rick Burke, combined the lightness of touch, the quick mind, and the metabolic resilience necessary to work for somebody like Kennedy, who never had hesitated to jerk any employee out of bed at three in the morning. "I'm just getting used to the idea that I can now be certain that I will come down my staircase to prepare breakfast and not find Edward Kennedy sitting in a living room chair, waiting for my husband to appear," insists the wife of one former aide. Employees deserve no private existence, partly because Kennedy doesn't.

The costs of public life are levied in private. Once the presidency loomed I remembered one afternoon, just as the Christmas recess of 1974-75 ended, when I stopped by and Kennedy invited me to join him as he walked over to the floor of the Senate to answer a roll call. Not that long before, his oldest son Teddy had lost a leg to ligament cancer, and there was still very little hope. "You know," Kennedy told a friend soon after the diagnosis was made, "I understand that there are perhaps fifty children in the United States with this thing. And I've got one." He'd shaken his head.

We took the shuttle car that runs the tunnel between the Senate office buildings and the Capitol, and nobody brought up young Teddy's struggle. Inside the elevator were Lowell Weicker and George McGovern and explosive hard-bitten

Strom Thurmond, whose puckered old pate was stippled just then with the liver-colored dots of his very recent hair transplant.

"Senator," Thurmond said, and with obvious sincerity, "Ah was awful sorry to hear about your boy. Ah know what that can do to a kid. Ah got a chile, know what Ah mean? Last summer he got this terrible dah-a-ree-a."

Kennedy nodded, saying nothing. The big muscles at the hinge of his jaw started cording. "It was awful," Thurmond said. "Your boy ever get dah-a-ree-a, Senator?"

"He—"

"Well, that's what mah son got himself. And it lasted a lot of the summer, too. So Ah know what you're goin' through."

Kennedy didn't say anything.

That winter, and for the next eighteen months, Kennedy and his son took on a kind of ritual agony which may have affected them both as deeply as anything in their lives. Every three weeks, first in Children's Hospital in Boston, then later in Washington, they underwent a weekend alone together, throughout most of which the thirteen-year-old Teddy was in and out of paroxysms of intense nausea from intravenous ingestion of an extremely powerful methotrexate compound, which researchers felt offered what hope there was. This was not great. "It's all very much like picking up coffee grounds with a sponge," Kennedy told one intimate. "You can scrape and scrape. But unless you get every last cell there's no point." The drug cost two thousand dollars per treatment, a figure Kennedy himself would later bring up in hearings to underline the final medical resorts open to the rich but denied everybody else.

In Washington, Kennedy learned to administer Teddy's follow-up injections, and spent what time he could encouraging his son. "It was very rough," he said soon afterward. "Very, very rough. He's a courageous boy, but it is very tough, the whole thing. Starting with the process of telling a child that he is about to lose a leg." The fact that Teddy did survive and appears to have managed a cure still seems a dispensation. "The silver streak in that grim and difficult time is that it has formed a bond between him and me that has just been . . . extraordinary. I can't tell whether it would have been so or not otherwise." This livened Kennedy up, and he was quickly launched on a description of how his son subsequently learned to ski with one leg — twenty yards and fall the first day, fifty yards the next. "Having measured up to that particular process I find in Teddy a great sense of assurance, of self-worth," Kennedy says. "He is a very sensitive boy, but in an upbeat way. He takes a lot of time with people; he's very interested. He's personable. At least I find him that way."

Kennedy still called home most days to assure his children that nobody had killed him yet. The youngest child, Patrick, was far enough gone with asthma to sleep in an iron lung much of the time, and often carried inhalation equipment. The eldest, Kara, was reportedly terrified of "catching" her brother's cancer, and — encouraged by one of the many household employees who were forever hiring on and resigning — ameliorated the strain with grass and hash. There was a period during which she ran away repeatedly, sometimes to one of the county-run "safe homes," where somebody would telephone the senator, who then would arrive, red-faced and furious with the local authorities, to pick Kara up. "Teddy's illness was such a traumatic event," Kennedy admits with reference to Kara. "The center, the attention went entirely to him."

And as for Joan? "She spent a lot of time with Teddy," Kennedy says, very quietly. "She felt better during that period." Joan notes this also. "I remember about four and a half years ago, when my son Teddy had his leg amputated, I didn't take a drink. I was in okay shape while he was in the hospital. I was the mother by the bedside. But as soon as he was well and back in school, I just collapsed. I needed some relief from having to be so damn brave all the time."

This quotation is directly from Joan Braden's long interview with Joan Kennedy in the August 1978 *McCall's*. That Joan might speak — might now be permitted to speak — so publicly of matters which, while alluded to often enough these days even in the respectable press, had never been commented on officially, does suggest a wholesale and deliberate emptying of emotional attics.

Acquaintances saw this coming. One, a long-standing journalist friend of the Kennedy family, remembers stopping at Kennedy's house in Hyannis Port to talk and have a drink. As he was leaving, Kennedy suggested that the visitor hadn't had a chance yet to say hello to Joan, and led him around to the back of the house; Joan lay crumpled up, passed out in the back seat of one of the Kennedy cars. "She was a rag mop," the friend observes. "I've seen drunks often enough, but what I was looking at there was the result of a two- or three-day bender. I think Kennedy just wanted me to see what he was up against. If something got printed, he was prepared for that."

The most poignant of Joan Kennedy's remarks concerned her failure to discuss her terrifying alcohol problem with her husband: "I tried to talk about it but I was embarrassed and Ted was embarrassed about it." This lasted a decade at least. "The Irish can do that with great distinction," says one old-timer, who knows the Kennedys well. "They just part slowly, and nobody can talk about it. Divorce is unthinkable; nobody can say it. The shorthand system takes over. 'I'm going out with the boys,' or 'I'm going on a political trip.' And she can't say 'You're going out to get laid' or something. And then it's over; it ends without a shot being fired."

Blame must be laid in part on the accumulated effects of overwork, of over-scheduling, on the "stresses" — an important word to Joan those days — that piled up when experts crowded in so often at dinner time, and aides stayed over, and hour after hour the conversation revolved around technical details or matters of legislative strategy — in which Joan manifested, at best, a dutiful passing interest. As Joan blanked out, or put in time at sanitariums like Silver Hill, Kennedy himself took over, showed up at junior high assemblies and squeezed in sledding afternoons and interludes of kickball with the youngsters. Joan became an onlooker; the beauty in the photographs around their houses had come to differ so markedly from the sad, swollen, preoccupied forty-year-old who still might appear that visitors felt haunted. In the summer of 1977 Joan joined Alcoholics Anonymous and took the pledge, and shortly after that she moved to Boston and started working toward a degree in music at Lesley graduate school, with the intention of teaching. She gradually stopped drinking.

"People ask whether newspaper stories about Ted and girls hurt my feelings," Joan told Braden. "Of course they hurt my feelings. They went to the core of my self-esteem." There is a nakedness to this no rationalizations can cover.

Yet this too requires some enlargement of the frame. Nobody anywhere near Kennedy would deny his susceptibility throughout the seventies to interested ladies across the political and social circuit. Every profession involves hazards, and combed-out young women with history on their minds are just as omnipresent at political functions as chafing-dish hot dogs, bubbling in their sauces. Kennedy was not raised to abstain, and evidence is rare that he did. "The senator would like to take you home tonight," Bo Burlingham quotes Richard Goodwin, secondhand, approaching a recalcitrant young female journalist at a Cambridge party, soon after the senator had bestowed on her a "very intense, very meaningful stare." She reportedly declined, but not everybody would.

What sometimes ruffled Kennedy is how much people build this into. "Where'd you get that, *Human Events*?" Kennedy snarled over television some years ago when one of the panelists alluded to the senator's publicized conquests. When a celebrated companion flew east and actually presented herself at the Old Senate Office Building, Kennedy cued an assistant with one meaningful sideways gesture of the eyes the moment his visitor turned away: Get her out of here! This was, after all, Kennedy's place of business. Not very long afterward a friend of some years' standing went after Kennedy about all the notoriety the relationship involved. The senator appeared perplexed. "What difference does it make? I'm not in love with her," he responded at once.

That would be quite another matter. If it be better to marry than to burn, a one-night stand every once in a while may warrant the sanctity of marriage. So much about life had become warding off collapse.

3

In September of 1978 I came by Kennedy's hideaway office just off the dome of the capitol to interview him for a magazine piece. I well remember watching him slump there, squirming to get comfortable, while against the small of his aching back he worked the fingers of one freckled hand to adjust just right the warmth of his heating pad. Its bright, obvious cord trailed alongside the sprawl of a trouser leg and into an outlet someplace behind his battered, buttoned love seat. There was a stack of file folders piled up next to him, from which his Benjamin Franklin glasses kept threatening to slide each time he reached out to gesture with his fingertips. Kennedy would be forty-seven in February, on George Washington's birthday, and accordingly had been alive longer than any of his brothers. Primogeniture had reversed itself and left him senior to them all.

The back hurt; the senator kept boosting himself gingerly to offset the pain. His weight was up just then; each exertion produced bulges. The alarm buzzer sounded, signaling a vote, and Kennedy made use of the delay the noise required by dredging up the remains of a cigar; his mottled brick jowls worked heavily to reignite it. Those hooded eyes — blood-flagged — strayed back into focus. I forget between visits how supernaturally large Kennedy's face invariably looks to me.

Suddenly the buzzer stops; I attempt another question; Kennedy's honeyed explanation continues. There is, as always, a tendency to leave himself out of his commentary, to sidestep personal involvement. "I suppose at different times in the political experience that you have conflicts, and you learn soon that those you oppose one day you are going to work very closely with on another. Otherwise your effectiveness around here is very limited," he remarks, with reference to Bobby Byrd. Or — regarding Carter — "We've got some . . . uh . . . areas of difference." But mostly the answers are responsive and satisfying — sharp, complete, overlaying point after point with background and precision. We discuss the crime bill, the health bill, the snares and gratification's involved with working alongside the Carter administration.

In fact, as soon as Carter became a feasible candidate in 1976 there had been bull-of-the-herd exchanges. As early as May that year Kennedy had pointedly refused to meet with the front-runner in Washington, then lambasted Carter for appearing "indefinite and imprecise" on critical issues, to which the Georgian responded — precise on this point — "I don't have to kiss his ass." Then Carter got elected; in Washington, Kennedy's broad shadow fell across a disheartening amount of government business. Carter's kiss planted early would soon look cheap at the price.

Their rivalry kept surfacing over health insurance. More than any other, this was Kennedy's issue. As chairman since 1971 of the forerunner of the Subcommittee on Health and Scientific Research of the Human Resources Committee, Kennedy decided years ago that anything short of comprehensive, mandatory national coverage couldn't meet public needs.

Slogging through the primaries, Jimmy Carter had kept his own thoughts on the subject largely to himself until his candidacy looked serious. Then — after meetings with labor, whose support he'd require — Carter went so far as to propose that: "rates for institutional care and physician services should be set in advance, prospectively."

After Carter became president his interest in health insurance dampened. Kennedy brooded all spring, and then on May 17, 1977, before the United Auto Workers in Los Angeles, he stressed that "health reform" was already in danger of becoming the "missing promise" of the new administration. The shock registered instantly; the next day, also before the Auto Workers, President Carter declared that he intended to have the administration's bill ready before the end of 1978.

Throughout the previous autumn Kennedy had been collaborating very closely with Douglas Fraser, president of the United Auto Workers, who like other labor leaders regarded health with close to single-issue intensity. Fraser brought new energy to Walter Reuther's Committee for National Health Insurance, which enlisted the groups in America Kennedy refers to as "underrepresented elements" — old people, clerics, farmers, nurses, minorities. With Hubert Humphrey dead, Kennedy became the spokesman in Congress for millions of bypassed citizens. Such coalitions are underfinanced, temporary, and fragile, but it was Kennedy's perception that this could hold together — and pick up legislative majorities — if he and Carter could agree on language in time.

There were personnel problems: Kennedy respected Stuart Eizenstat, who represented the White House, but he was badly put off by lackadaisical Georgia staffers. "Ted is so tough on staff, he just doesn't tolerate sloppy staff work," said one observer. "I think he thinks Carter has some awful chowderheads around."

Negotiations made slow headway; a date of Friday, July 28, was set to announce the details; unexpectedly, on July 18, Eizenstat dropped in on Kennedy's health staff director Larry Horowitz to leave a draft of what the administration expected. Kennedy and his people were dumbfounded. They'd gone along with the administration's $20-billion-a-year initial projection, a skeletal bureaucracy, a continuing role for private insurers. They'd conceded a maximum of discretion on the executive side in implementing stages of the program — a two-year start-up period, with benefits phased in through 1983, 1985, 1987. Now Carter reserved for the president a sequence of "trigger devices" to abort any phase of the program should factors in the economy make health spending undesirable. This arbitrary a procedure was unthinkable to Fraser. "The next morning Kennedy went in and saw Carter to urge that they stick together on the issue," Horowitz says. "Carter wouldn't budge."

Kennedy braced for confrontation. Just before the administration was scheduled to release its bill, Kennedy telephoned Califano to alert the secretary that he had decided to mount his own press conference on July 28, and that he expected to attack the Carter plan. Perhaps Califano might present the administration's ideas first. The alarmed president summoned Kennedy in hopes of compromise. Too late: Kennedy seized the headlines, flanked on the podium by an array of church, farm, and labor leaders headed by George Meany.

The president was guilty, Kennedy proclaimed, of a "failure of leadership," which now threatened to "make our efforts more difficult in the future." He and his subcommittee would proceed with hearings on their own. As for the Carter proposal? "The groups of elderly and the labor unions are still for our plan," he told a reporter after a few days. "The Senate

Finance Committee is supporting a bill limited to catastrophic illness, but as for Carter, I don't know who's supporting his bill."

"I don't myself question the motives of the president," Kennedy explained to me soon afterward. "I think he felt that he would be able to set in motion a series of bills whose outcome would be the same as ours. My own sense was — after sixteen years in the Senate — that the House and the Senate would pass the easiest part of this bill, and leave it." The inflated red face looked melancholy, pouting. "Our feeling, of course, is that health care is a right. If this is conditioned on a set of circumstances, that really isn't a right at all."

In December of 1978, visiting Memphis, the aroused Massachusetts senator was far enough along to share his alarms and excursions with delegates to Carter's hand-picked Democratic National Conference. One palm stretched reassuringly above the expectant crowd, Kennedy harangued this sea of organization regulars for "policy that cuts spending to the bone in areas like jobs and health," while promoting "greater fat and waste through inflationary spending for defense." The tumult was dumbfounding. "We went down there just to fire a shot across the bow," one Kennedy aide admitted. "We did not expect the depth and intensity of the reaction."

Carter reacted clumsily. The Massachusetts senator's "special aura of appreciation," he told a press conference, owed much to the "position of his family in our nation and in our party." This cut to Kennedy's self-esteem. This was becoming personal.

By then Kennedy was marshaling the talents of a staff that approached one hundred top people once he became Judiciary chairman. He moved without apology into areas of statecraft with little or nothing to do with legitimate committee assignments.

Take foreign policy. Shortly before we talked that September of 1978 Kennedy had appeared in Russia to attend a United Nations health conference and to converse at extraordinary length with Soviet President Brezhnev. This offstage baby summit, not Kennedy's first, was leisurely but effective: the senator was concerned, he said, in putting over "one senator's views" to ease the after-effects of the Carter State Department's blundering reformulation of the all-but-complete SALT II agreements. This might be particularly useful now, Kennedy felt, since Carter hadn't bothered to take anybody in Congress with him to Vienna. Kennedy's involvement was predicated on "private assurances" by his hosts that the show trial of International Harvester representative Francis Jay Crawford for currency violations wouldn't embarrass this visitor. Before Kennedy left Moscow Crawford had been let go, and eighteen dissident Jewish families were permitted to emigrate.

Within the Senate itself, Kennedy had consistently operated solidly to the left of Carter on shifting international problem areas. Kennedy amendments on Chile and Argentina terminated resupply of military equipment to their governments on grounds of gross violations of human rights. "He was a major player," one insider observes, "throughout the crises in Nicaragua and the Dominican Republic."

Kennedy's readiness to shadow — and bypass — the administration became apparent over China. China was Kennedy's issue — he proposed some measure of relations with the People's Republic as early as 1967, and stood by enthusiastically when Kissinger approached the mainland. Carter neglected China; in January of 1978 Kennedy took his family to Peking, met Deng Xiao-Ping, and returned to prod the administration.

On December 15, abruptly, Carter announced the establishment of regular diplomatic relations with the People's Republic, along with his decision to allow the mutual defense treaty with Taiwan to lapse. The whirlwind was anticipated: the China Lobby reared, and Barry Goldwater immediately threatened to sue the president for infringing on Senate prerogatives.

On January 25, 1979, presiding over a quiet dinner for eighteen that was overlooked by the press, Kennedy invited to his home in McLean a delegation of mainland Chinese led by the new Chinese ambassador, His Excellency Chai Tse-min. Also present were Assistant Secretary of State Richard Holbrooke, Ambassador Woodcock, a member of the National Security Council, and Senators Culver, Cranston, Glenn, Percy, Bentsen, and Bayh. Sometime during the evening, obviously by prearrangement, Foreign Relations member Percy sounded out the ambassador from China on a proposed Kennedy-Cranston Resolution, the gist of which was manifestly the proviso "Whereas the United States recognizes that an armed attack directed against Taiwan would represent a danger to the stability and peace of the area." Should aggression occur, the resolution proceeded, "The President is directed to inform the Congress promptly."

With a historic wink, Chai Tse-min indicated that he foresaw no problem, since "Whatever comes out must be consistent with normalization." Sponsored by colleagues ranging from McGovern to Hayakawa, the Taiwan Relations Act went on the books in March, welcomed, Kennedy China expert Jan Kalicki noted, "by the Chinese on both sides of the Taiwan Strait."

The president wasn't impressed. "The so-called Kennedy-Cranston resolution," he indicated, was a diplomatic redundancy. At about this period Carter's Attorney General Griffin Bell highlighted White House sentiment. "The President . . . asked me the other day if I thought Senator Kennedy would accept an appointment to the Supreme Court. I replied that I did not believe he would want to give up being co-president."

Kennedy had been coy, comparatively, second-guessing the administration about Taiwan. Regarding energy policy, over which he plastered Carter's decision-making all spring, Kennedy opened up freely. As chairman of the Joint Economic Committee's Subcommittee on Energy as well as a primary mover on Judiciary inside the watchdog Subcommittee on Antitrust, Monopoly and Business Rights, the Massachusetts senior senator was as knowledgeable as anybody at either end of Pennsylvania Avenue concerning oil and the corporations.

Kennedy's complaint was twofold. With time and politics, Kennedy banged away, Carter and his Department of Energy turned all the way around on commitments central to his support in 1976. Carter had pledged to oppose deregulation of old oil and natural gas not under existing contracts, to prohibit horizontal energy monopolies, to expedite a strategic petroleum reserve, to downplay atomic reactors. Administration policy had worked toward precisely the opposite ends in virtually every case, compounding treachery with blunders like pouring 92 million barrels of oil into salt domes without providing for equipment to pump it out, ignoring enormous refinery profits that flouted Carter's announced guidelines, "bungling" gas negotiations with Mexico. To conservation — by 1979 a Kennedy keystone — Carter rendered "lip service."

In April of 1979 the president announced his decision to deregulate domestic oil reserves in phases through 1981. This move was unconditional, Carter admitted, although he was hoping for some kind of industry quid pro quo. Kennedy erupted publicly. The petroleum industry, he charged at once, had "intimidated the Administration into throwing in the towel without even entering the ring on the issue of price decontrol. And second, it has also intimidated the Administration into submitting a token windfall tax that is no more than a transparent fig leaf over the vast new profits the industry will reap."

"Baloney," Carter responded. Kennedy's willingness to rubber-stamp Jimmy Carter's presidency was reaching historically low levels.

4

On May 2, 1979, just leaving the White House after a Law Day ceremony, Kennedy brushed off reporters who wondered whether Carter's recent decisions affected Kennedy's own prospects. "I've indicated that I expect the president to be a candidate," he muttered in passing.

"Does that mean Kennedy would not seek the presidency?"

"I can use my own words as well as yours or anybody else's," the Massachusetts senator snapped.

Could this be happening? "How can I run for the presidency, for God's sake?" Kennedy asked one intimate in 1974. "I'd have to do it with my back to the wall, and these days there isn't even a wall behind me anymore." He'd meant his immediate family; now relations were stabilizing. There were emotional considerations. "Right!" he told an acquaintance who remarked, on a transcontinental coach flight as 1978 was ending, that if he ever did become president he'd get a proper seat on Air Force One. "Planes. Airplanes and the telephones — that's just what Bobby used to say, those are the two great benefits of the presidency." He'd rearranged to stretch his back a little. "Otherwise, you can have the goddamned job," Edward Kennedy said.

By 1979 a well-positioned Democrat summed up: "All spring and summer people were coming to Senator Kennedy, people he had known for a long time, and they were saying: this administration is dangerous. It has no goals, it has no policies, it has no juices, it has no organization, it has no consistent positions, it has no leaders. It acts out of confusion, out of desperation, out of panic, it acts out of short-run political and legislative goals induced by a very fleeting set of tactics. It set itself up into positions where it is totally vulnerable to the opposite of what it started out to get in the first place, and then it calls getting the opposite of what it started out to get as somehow a victory." In short, utter chaos.

Other voices Kennedy heard reflected career concerns. In 1980 an extraordinary number of Democratic senators — twenty-four — many liberal, came up for election — an exposure that threatened the party with minority status for the first time since 1952. "There was a great deal of talk at the time that the Democrats would lose the Senate," Carey Parker recalled in 1979. Kennedy's balding, circumspect legislative assistant then took this one step closer to a hint: "A lot of committee chairmen were nervous."

According to one senator who expected a fight to retain his seat in 1980, "various labor people were going around," who "came to me, to urge the people that were up in '80 to urge Ted to run." The energetic Al Barkan, head bouncer for the AFL-CIO's Committee on Political Education, pops up in several conversations; one source very close to Kennedy maintains that anti-Carter feeling among the major union chieftains was running so strong at this point that the message Kennedy got was "Prepare to move now, or forget about us in 1984." The endorsement by Winpisinger of the Machinists was primarily the testing edge. Auto Workers, Graphic Artists, Government Employees got ready.

Kennedy heard all this, daily, spreading. Reverberations reached the White House; the gizzardy little president reacted. He red-penciled Kennedy's recommendation that Archibald Cox go onto the Court of Appeals, potentially a costly veto to inflict on a Judiciary Committee chairman when 152 federal judgeships, a full third, were up for appointment. In June of 1979 the president himself enunciated the White House position on the subject. "If Kennedy runs," he told a delegation of badly startled congressmen, "I'll whip his ass."

"I always knew the White House would stand behind me," Kennedy responded, "but I didn't realize how close they would be." This broke him up. Then — allowing himself one step — "If I were to run, which I don't intend to, I would hope to win."

This perception of himself as critic — on occasion, with veto powers — of ongoing presidential policy Edward Kennedy came by naturally. Virtually from the day he intervened to sweet-talk William Randolph Hearst into conceding the vital California delegation to Franklin Roosevelt in 1932, the founder Joseph P. Kennedy had arrogated for himself at the very least a *consulting* role in White House decision-making. When Roosevelt was on the point of easing the general embargo of arms to Spain in 1938 — a move well calculated to save the Loyalists from the Nazi-equipped Franco — Kennedy marshaled the pressure group that forestalled the shift.

Kennedy's influence over contemporary Democratic isolationists was so great, the authoritative Ted Morgan concludes, that "FDR . . . sent Joe Kennedy to London, wanting him out of the country rather than lending his talents to the conservative wing of the party." Morgan quotes Roosevelt as characterizing Joe as "a very dangerous man," and adding that "I have made arrangements to have Joe Kennedy watched hourly and the first time he opens his mouth and criticizes me, I will fire him."

Joe himself kept current the rumors of his availability for a draft as the Democratic nominee, backing off characteristically at the ultimate moment (when counterpressure from FDR's ramrods became unendurable), followed up by a frothy public endorsement to placate his crafty boss in the White House. To justify such repeated changes of heart, in 1940 Joe divulged to intimates like Arthur Krock that Roosevelt had privately knuckled under and pledged to support *him* as a presidential candidate in 1944 if he got behind FDR's unprecedented third term. Joe's ambition died hard, and then was off-loaded onto his boys.

To become the president came down as part of the legacy, the fulfillment of the old Ambassador's ultimate pretensions. He was never one to depend to any extent on hope. Tip O'Neill once raised his glass to me and confided that he himself had trouped the nation's courthouses, as soon as John Kennedy came into contention in 1960, as the founding father's designated bagman, sallying forth on several occasions with a thick roll of hundred-dollar bills pressed into his palm by the financier personally for holdouts like Mike DiSalle of Ohio. In Wisconsin initially, and later in West Virginia, the Kennedy millions blanketed the media and swamped the challenger Hubert Humphrey. While Hubert rattled along in a smelly rented bus, Jack Kennedy flew comfortably in a fitted-out Convair, leased back from a family company to avoid listing as a campaign contribution. Jack himself would joke about a wire from his father cautioning him not to buy "one vote more than necessary. I'll be damned if I'll pay for a landslide." In fact, where it would make a difference, the Ambassador hadn't hesitated to part with whatever it took.

Once Jack got elected, old Joe slipped behind the arras but insisted on installing Bobby — "a great kid, he hates the same way I do," the Ambassador once remarked — as Attorney General. Bobby amounted to old Joe's understudy. Jack attempted to keep his hard-nosed younger brother out of the decision-making until the collective loss of nerve which erupted after the Bay of Pigs forced Jack to bring Bobby in as a kind of general-purpose clerk-of-the-works. After Jack was shot, Bobby had hung on disconsolate and increasingly isolated within the Johnson administration into 1964, his claims to policy involvement laughable in the face of Lyndon's undisguised distaste. Then it became unendurable, and Bobby fell victim to a Johnson purge and reconstituted himself as a senator from New York.

Johnson went on as president, and Robert Kennedy now took it upon himself to monitor the Johnson administration. The truth was, the advisors around Johnson — Joe Califano, Bill Moyers, Jack Valenti, Clark Clifford — all tended to favor an agenda a lot more radical and populist in thrust than Kennedy ever had. Jack had been cool, moderate, skittish at the prospect that anybody might tag him as a liberal. Accused once of not being a "true liberal," John Kennedy remarked that "I'd be very happy to tell them I'm not a liberal at all." He had

been backed unhappily into calling up federal marshals to en-
force university entrance requirements in Alabama. Johnson,
leaning on his one-time colleagues and breathing very hard,
jockeyed through the fundamental Civil Rights and Voting
Rights legislation which were to provide legal bedrock to our
emerging multiracial society.

But Johnson was misguided enough to invest in and expand
the war in Vietnam. The war had without question come down
from the Kennedy administration, which deployed the first
U.S. detachments on the ground in serious numbers; Robert
Kennedy — spurred on by the theories of his mentor, Maxwell
Taylor — had designated himself spokesman for counterinsur-
gency among his brother's advisors.

By the middle sixties Bobby recognized his mistake. The
war was polarizing society; Johnson was mired in. Like Joe
Kennedy second-guessing FDR throughout the Battle of Brit-
ain, Robert Kennedy now turned himself into an increasingly outspoken center of opposition to the Vietnam war. He'd
begun to discover his ultimate constituency.

Bobby's kid brother, Ted, wasn't all that sure. A lifetime as
anchor man at the far end of the Kennedy lineup couldn't help
but condition his development as a freshman senator. He'd
been a toy, the butt of too many jokes among his avid siblings,
a doughty little celebrity at six when all the flashbulbs went off
at Buckingham Palace and he was included too, their pudgy
little last-born in his Buster Brown cap accommodating life on
foreign soil.

Something of an afterthought in this clan of quick-witted
opportunists, Kennedy sensed the strength of consistency, the
long-range payoff that might come with taking a political
stand, defining for himself a political role solid enough to out-
last the headlines of a season. The others had worked for theirs,

but celebrity *broke* over Edward Kennedy, he found it thrust upon him early. It made him nervous underneath, a lot more answerable than he wanted to be for everything people caught him at.

Driven hard every minute, Ted Kennedy's personal identity would take decades to coalesce. By contrast his political identity formed early, deepened steadily. He remained an heir to the aspirations of the New Deal Left, a tribune of the helpless, the nation's social conscience.

By the later sixties Edward Kennedy had begun to identify his place in the Senate. He was not nearly as squeamish at being labeled a man of the left as Jack or the early Bobby, and ideologically he would soon emerge as more the heir of Hubert Humphrey and Lyndon Johnson than of his brother, the president. Johnson got along with Ted personally, and visited him in 1964 in the hospital after his plane crashed. Ted's deepest prompting almost to the end remained to avoid confronting a sitting Democratic president.

But Bobby was hardening. "Am I still interested in getting Jimmy Hoffa?" I heard him snap once, all viscous gutturals, to one old friend at a noisy family gathering shortly before he declared himself. Some retainer was passing around those inedible sandwiches the Kennedys appear to favor. "Why would I worry about him when I've got Lyndon to work on?"

So this was nothing new, challenging the White House. By 1979 Edward Kennedy had come to it slowly, activated in good part by his perception that Jimmy Carter was selling liberals out, and partly by a panic spreading among the regulars that Carter was collapsing in the polls, he couldn't win reelection, he'd take the Party down with him. That, and perhaps a twitch somewhere in Kennedy's genetic memory to remind him that this was expected of him before he died.

———

People closest to Kennedy agree that he let his presidential decision drift until the summer recess, but it was there by September. By that time Jimmy Carter's slide looked irrecoverable, too steep to make an issue out of splitting the party. His public approval rate hit 19 percent. The draft-Kennedy movements were already picking up steam. Carter's down-from-the-mountain shakeup, which cost the strongest of the Cabinet members jobs, looked beyond desperation, at least to Kennedy. "He was especially annoyed at the way they booted Joe Califano," one close aide stressed. "The senator felt that Califano was an able and competent Cabinet officer, into some very good things. They needed a scapegoat, somebody to blame, and there was reason to believe that Califano's anti-smoking policies had alienated the powers-that-be in North Carolina, which the White House thought it needed for re-election. So they fired Joe. The senator felt that was not the way to run a government."

Phases of his thinking could easily be plotted. By early spring, responding to *Boston Globe* veteran Robert Healy, the senator did concede that if and when Carter decided to relinquish a second term, he himself would have to think "terribly seriously" about what to do. This ignited the wires. Such bits in political code became commoner and commoner. He let in reporters that summer and talked about Chappaquiddick. Kennedy's back was manageable; an ulcer had healed, and there was no concern now after a skin cancer excision. He'd gotten his weight down, finally. Kara, and now Teddy, were enrolled in college in Connecticut. "I saw him the day after the August recess," divulged one colleague, who had asked Kennedy whether he might attend a 1980 fund-raiser in his state. "He said, 'Well, I'll do anything I can. But let's wait until things sort out a bit.' That, to me, was the first concrete indication. Then, you know, Rose gave her blessing, and Joan gave hers, and after that it was The Week That Was. Every day there was some new revelation."

Ultimately Kennedy explained himself. "My father always said," he told one doubter, "'If it's on the table, eat it.'" He scheduled his announcement of candidacy for November 7, as soon as political decency allowed after the October 20 opening of the Kennedy Library. Jimmy Carter was expected to give the dedicatory speech.

Carter had an undertaker's touch, reporters wrote afterward, but hadn't the president demonstrated a lot more style at that then all those grabby Kennedys combined? The way he jibbed Teddy by quoting Jack at him about waiting his turn? Punchy! The box score opened: one Carter, zilch to the challenger. Onlookers were already screaming for an early knockdown.

More insidious — and more damaging — was the nationwide fallout from the CBS documentary "Teddy," written and reported by Roger Mudd. The hour was culled from the network's recent coverage of the senator; its tone and movement came out of clips that Mudd had selected after several long interviews, one on September 29 at Hyannis Port, to which the senator had agreed before he decided to run.

Mudd set Kennedy up. Half of the air time directly involved Chappaquiddick; the montage of shots of the bridge and the overturned Oldsmobile alternated with questions he'd answered again and again over the preceding decade. Frustrated and coldly angry, Mudd concluded that "It is now obvious that Kennedy and his advisers plan to volunteer nothing more on Chappaquiddick, or make any attempt to clear away the lingering contradictions." He had already upset Kennedy by referring to Kennedy's marriage as one that existed "only on selected occasions," to which the senator responded, badly thrown off:

"Well, I think that — it's a — it's had some difficult times, but I think we have — we, I think have been able to make some very good progress and it's — I would say that it's — delighted to share the time and the relationship that we, that we do share." Although admitting that Kennedy was indeed a "first-class senator," Mudd explained that away by characterizing him as a "captive of his bushy-tailed staff," and demonstrated this dependence with a sequence showing Kennedy greeting a congressman by his first name a moment after an aide whispered a name into the senator's ear. Mudd bored away openly at Kennedy's reputation as a skirt chaser, and dealt with Joan's alcohol problem, to which the shaken Kennedy himself referred.

With Kennedy scheduled to announce his candidacy on November 7, CBS broadcast the documentary early, on Sunday night, November 4, opposite *Jaws*. Late in October, according to a close Kennedy aide, the network "released the transcript" — with all Kennedy's emotional staggerings rendered on the page — "to the White House, who gave it to the reporters three days before it ran. It reads a lot worse than it looks." The first round of columnists taking off on Kennedy was based on these; Kennedy's initial drop registered.

The image of Kennedy to emerge from Mudd's documentary overwhelmed the journalistic community. A disgusted Jimmy Breslin proposed that Kennedy start out by establishing: "I'm no good and I can prove it." Much of this translated into weakening political results. Florida's premature "preferential convention" opted one-sidedly for the president. A Democratic National Committee straw poll favored Carter over Brown or Kennedy. An uncommonly seductive president showed up in Chicago, and only a last-minute appeal to decency turned Chicago mayor Jane Byrne around in time.

Liberals who could count — Rick Stearns from the Mc-Govern operation, disillusioned Carter speechwriter Robert Shrum, Eddie Martin, Jim Flug, Peter Edelman from Bobby's old staff — joined Kennedy almost immediately. Before November was finished Ted Kennedy was rolling across the hustings to demand that his party help him "end twelve years of Republican rule and put a real Democrat in the White House." Meanwhile — quietly — Kennedy hardened on defense issues.

There were dangerous ifs.

If nobody blasted Kennedy.

If Joan remained stable.

So far she'd responded. At the library dedication she certainly seemed merry enough, her hair like straw before that prevailing Dorchester wind. The television batteries picked up on Joan plucking for a moment at Jimmy Carter's sleeve, giggling at an aside, while on her other flank her husband waited set-lipped. Local reporters noted that Joan had apparently forgotten her wedding ring someplace in the apartment.

Yet several weeks afterward, summoned to the rostrum at Faneuil Hall to second her husband's candidacy, she looked a masterpiece of overnight political restoration. Tailored perfectly in violet, doe-eyed again and aglow with makeup, her hair two spun-gold fronds to frame that vulnerable sensitive chin. "I look forward very very enthusiastically to my husband being a candidate," Joan opened. Her quavering voice guttered; she clutched the rostrum. "Soon," she resumed shortly, "I will be talking with members of the press and at that time I hope to answer all of your questions that you might have on your minds today." Behind Joan, unremarked, little Patrick wept quietly.

Public life, and private. The year before, struggling to explain all this at least to himself, Kennedy observed to me in rather a humbled tone, "The more I discover about other people's personal lives the more I see that every household has . . . problems, in one form or another. People do the best they can."

It came to this: the politics of compassion. "I suspect people feel a lot of that," one veteran Washingtonian remarked at the time. "They pick it up just looking at Kennedy and listening to his voice — the vibrating warmth, even the garbagy side. I have a feeling that's part of the reason for his tremendous strength in the polls. Their lives are shambles, and they know he's taken his share. He's a known quantity, familiar, and they can sense that like all great leaders he identifies with them."

5

The euphoria around Kennedy persisted almost until the day he announced his candidacy. Then and now, analysts trace the first true crack in the campaign to the airing of Kennedy's November 4, 1979 CBS interview with Roger Mudd. There would be charges that Mudd deliberately blindsided Kennedy, that Mudd remained affected in some obscure way by memories of Mary Jo Kopechne, that by exploiting a merciless pattern of editing and intercutting he intended to demonstrate to his peers that despite his membership in Ethel Kennedy's entourage he had kept himself unbeholden to Ted. But even Kennedy's intimates were startled at the way the senator stumbled and temporized throughout, unnerved by personal questions and unable to explain with any coherence his own motives in seeking the presidency. "It was like, I want to be president because the sea is so deep and the sky is so blue," Mudd observed afterward.

Rocked by the Mudd interview, Kennedy formalized his candidacy late in November of 1979 and launched into barnstorming. Early weeks were headlong, strenuous, as if he expected to wrap it up in one furious round. Kennedy would later confess that he had spent much too much time attempting to decide whether he wanted to run, and not nearly enough establishing how. Yet frequently his manner seemed desultory and uncertain between bursts of rhetoric, as if he found himself shoved out onto the stage and suddenly seemed puzzled about what people expected. Whenever crowds responded listlessly he attempted to harangue them to life.

Quite often he lost track. "Roll up your sleeves and your mother and your fathers," he implored one audience in November. A week later, just as the hostage crisis was breaking in Teheran, the fatigued campaigner favored a late-evening radio interviewer with his opinion of the deposed Shah: "The Shah had the reins of power and ran one of the most violent regimes in the history of mankind — in the form of terrorism and the basic and fundamental violations of human rights, in the most cruel circumstances, to his own people. . . ." Why admit the Shah, "with his umpteen billions of dollars that he's stolen from Iran and, at the same time, say to Hispanics who are here legally that they have to wait nine years to bring their wife and children to this country."

This was a response which stunned the establishment, Republican and Democrat equally. Reza Pahlevi carried water for American policymakers in the Middle East since World War II ended, the CIA had manipulated him back into power in 1953. He may have been a sonovabitch, as FDR once phrased it, but he was *our* sonovabitch. Shortly afterward Kennedy press spokesman Tom Southwick confessed to "ayatollah dreams," during which his boss wrote Khomeini: "'Greetings, I will give my blood for you!'"

"Ted Kennedy is the worst politician I've ever seen in my life at saying nothing," Bob Shrum says — Shrum means by this the worst at suppressing his opinions — and when he censors himself his delivery gets so stilted audiences claw toward the exits. Kennedy alternated between bumbling around the issues and blurting what he really thought. Too often his impulses violated the public mood. Days after Jimmy Carter responded to the Soviet Union's invasion of Afghanistan with a grain embargo against Moscow, Kennedy denounced it as "unworkable and unfair" to the American farmer. Again, Jimmy Carter had gauged the popular current, while Kennedy was swept away. Kennedy's polls slipped — slowly those early weeks, and then in what David Broder characterized as a "dizzying downward spiral."

"What's wrong? I'm not going to list the things that are wrong — everything is wrong," one "hollow-eyed senior strategist" admitted; fourteen years later, another advisor who has been close to Kennedy for decades admits there were good reasons for such a dramatic turn. "Kennedy had been drafted by the power structure of the Democratic Party. At that point we were doing the homework we should have done in April, May, June. These people were appalled that we couldn't run a good campaign." Chappaquiddick details resurfaced. Figures who had been allied to the Kennedys for several political generations — Abe Ribicoff, Averell Harriman, ultimately John Glenn and even, in the end, John Culver — sidled over to back the president. Big Labor defected wholesale.

In the Iowa caucuses, where crowds seemed responsive, Kennedy lost 2-1. By then, Kennedy's advisors admit, the president, impregnable in the Rose Garden, was strategizing the hostage crisis perfectly. As the year played out, it won him the nomination and cost him the election. Carter took New Hampshire. Kennedy reached a point at which, struggling to avoid gaffes, he spoke so slowly that there were jokes about a

defective teleprompter. This was a Kennedy campaign, columnists wrote, without a Kennedy. The struggle to present himself
as a consensus candidate increasingly left him tongue-tied.
Kennedy's ulcer started bleeding again. Reporters dubbed his
entourage "The Bozo Zone."

By February a lot of the faultfinding devolved on Stephen
Smith. Smith, the dapper, hard-bitten scion of a Brooklyn tug-
boat fortune, had married Kennedy's sister Jean and ran Joe's
money out of a big suite in the Pan Am building. He assumed
by right the managerial role in Ted's campaign. To hired-
gun veterans of the McGovern drive in '72 like Carl Wagner
and Rick Stearns, the chain-smoking Kennedy brother-in-law
came over as too well-dressed, too sure of himself, and innocent of oncoming technology. Smith declined to designate a
single media advisor for months, and continued to press, by a
contemporary report, "outdated, anachronistic ideas on polling,
on advertising, on how television works." One consultant, Joe
Napolitan, subsequently told Smith his initial round of ads was
"an embarrassment, probably the worst television ever produced for a presidential candidate in American history." The
rising abortion issue left Smith uncharacteristically irresolute,
paralyzed in the face of zealots picketing clinics around the
country.

The problem was melding three generations of Kennedy advisors into something that worked. "More than anything else
Steve had a strong desire to protect Kennedy," Bob Shrum said
recently. "Between Iowa and the convention he was primarily
concerned that Kennedy not be damaged more than he already
had been. But at the beginning, when everybody thought he
was going to win and millions of people were jumping on the
ship, there might be twenty-eight people in the room and
everybody would have a vote."

This was a whole new generation of advisors in politics. Smith played it straight and tried to give everybody a hearing, but he was brusque and quick-tempered much of the time, and remained a hard sell. "I joined the campaign in November," Shrum says, "and somebody told me that he and I started to get along in world-record time. I started to get along with him in March, four months into things, once we were working together on media for New York." Sixties veterans like Ted Sorenson and Dick Goodwin were in and out.

For family reasons, replacing Steve was out of the question. By April, one insider divulged to a reporter, "Teddy just doesn't give Steve authority to make all the decisions and he keeps things back. He plays him off the boards a bit." The friction was heating up between the field operation and the headquarters, with more power gravitating every week to the relentless Paul Kirk, backed up by Larry Horowitz and Tony Podesta and Joe Crangle while Bob Shrum and Carey Parker stuck with the candidate and traded off the speechwriting.

Paul Kirk would later ascribe the chaos to their "abrupt start," which precluded the "anticipatory shopping or interviewing of people who just might get such a thing together. . . . It was in part the accident of timing. The first couple of attempts weren't satisfactory." They continued to reinvent the machine even as it ran away. Kennedy himself juggled twenty-hour days on the stump with stolen moments to edit his own speeches, horse-trade with primary state managers, sneak calls in to squeeze fresh cash from supporters.

After the autumn mudslide Smith was emphatically disinclined to deplete the family assets further to maintain the trappings of a juggernaut. The chartered United Airlines 727 gave way to a much smaller aircraft, which survivors still characterize as a "zoo," with everybody pitching fresh approaches while the polls plummeted. Reporters — their editors increasingly snappish because the Kennedy campaign billed twice as much as counterparts in either party — attempted to justify the costs by worming favors and divulgences out of Kennedy's malleable office manager Rick Burke.

Everybody aboard still alludes, in Shrum's words, to the candidate's "resilience and good temper, the way he dealt with all of us and mostly with himself under conditions under which most people would have buckled." Emerging from an interview with *The New York Times* editorial board during which Kennedy discovered that biographical information supplied by Shrum and Carey Parker was largely inaccurate, their boss had eased back into the tucks of his limousine to remark, "Listen, I will thank you two to let me make my own mistakes. As you may have noticed, I'm outstanding at that."

The eighteen and nineteen-hour days precluded the usual highballs, although Kennedy, revved up and impatient as ever with delays and frustrations, let down during breaks by eating too much. Shrum remembers how he and his boss could "devour a two-pound cheese fairly quickly, given the right circumstances." Shrum recalls grazing nonstop throughout one fourteen-hour plane ride on an Air New England charter, which they had rented to save money without anticipating refueling stops in Charleston, North Carolina and Indianapolis en route to an appearance in Kansas City. "As we were coming in the pilot couldn't find the airport, and Denny Shaw and Larry Horowitz and I stood crowded in the front of the plane trying to locate it on a road map."

Another factor to reckon with was the senator's unpredictable wife Joan, back on the tour primarily at her own instigation. Spotted around the hustings wearing "a loud plaid suit, a purple blouse, and eye shadow to match," Joan presented herself as a "very sophisticated lady," who had already met Mr. Brezhnev and the leaders of China, "all these things Mrs. Carter has not done yet." She rationalized the fact that she had lived alone in Boston the last two years as full of advantages. Left behind in McLean with Patrick, Ted had grown much closer to his son. If Ted *did* win, she expected to join him in the White House. Her relocation had facilitated "my journey back to health." "One of the side effects of her unnerving speeches," Mary McGrory wrote, "was that some people who did not like her husband liked him less after hearing her troubles. 'It's been therapy for her,' grumped a Kennedy supporter. 'But how does it help him?'"

The pounding he took in Iowa seemed somehow to loosen Ted up more than it undid him. He was assimilating fast. On January 28 he gave the speech at Georgetown which dragged the props in under his campaign, belatedly responding in the process to Roger Mudd's costly question as to why he was running for the office. "I believe we must not permit the dream of social progress to be shattered by those whose premises have failed," he summed it up toward the close. "We cannot permit the Democratic party to remain captive to those who have been so confused about its ideals."

He had already laced into the newly propounded "Carter Doctrine," which, with its open commitment to military intervention in the Persian Gulf, "offers defense contractors a bright future of expansion and profit." Kennedy preferred to start with obligations both ways between the United States and the Gulf powers, bartering military support for oil stability. He blamed President Carter directly for letting the Shah into the United States for treatment and thereby precipitating the hostage crisis. Rather than reenacting draft registration, Kennedy called for gas rationing, along with wage and price controls to bring the rampant inflation down. "I want to be the president who at last closes tax loopholes and tames monopoly . . . halts the loss of rural land to giant conglomerates . . . brings national health insurance to safeguard every family from the fear of bankruptcy due to illness."

One idea man at the center of Kennedy's campaign sensed another dynamic. "Once it became apparent in the polling data that all these nice calculations about whether you should or you shouldn't come out for price controls and the rest weren't going to affect the outcome one way or the other, you might as well just throw everything at it because you weren't at a point where it was even worth calculating risks anymore. So he just went and did that: the Georgetown speech was just the classic liberal speech." There wasn't any need, Kennedy felt, to propitiate the Democratic right. "Now he had found his voice, and he could talk the way he was used to talking. And people saw that it was authentic.

"But beyond that — and I wouldn't want this attributed to me — I have a personal hypothesis that he lacked confidence in his ability to be president, and one of the reasons why his performance improved so drastically was in inverse relationship to how much he thought he had a chance to be president. The less he thought he could win the better a candidate he was. Although members of his family thought his fear of being shot was his biggest fear. . . ."

Spring brought victories. Underfunded all the way, Kennedy won in New York, in Pennsylvania, in Connecticut and Rhode Island and in New Jersey and finally in California. This was a surprising showing but it was never enough. Furthermore, as one of Kennedy's handlers admitted afterward, "There are always in the second stage of the primaries a lot of people, party professionals, who just want to slow down the front runner for reasons of their own. So he benefited from the people who had decided to renominate Carter but weren't just going to hand it to him."

Kennedy continued to close, but Carter had the delegates. By the end of June the wheelhorses of the party were starting to drop by to urge Ted to let it go. He was damaging Carter. Instead, Kennedy pushed the Judiciary Committee to probe Billy Carter's dealings with the Libyan government. He challenged the president to release his delegates and open the convention up. Bob Shrum and Jimmy Flug especially continued to feast on dreams, and Kennedy sometimes speculated as to what might happen if the delegates succumbed en masse to the right chemistry, at the right moment.

On fumes of glory, several generations of Kennedyites coasted into Manhattan in August. Money was so short that Ted and Joan lived out of a suite they shared with Bob Shrum and Carey Parker. Flug, who had been trouble-shooting the campaign from Iowa to Maryland, had been installed as press secretary by Paul Kirk after Pennsylvania. At the convention itself "We had no budget whatsoever," Flug remembers. "The delegate operation had whatever money there was. So I was in charge of setting up the press operation. Installing lines is very expensive, especially in New York. We had a press room in the hotel, and a press room in the garden. I did not pay for one phone. I had a bank of pay phones in each place. The press people we liked we gave the incoming numbers for the pay phones."

It wasn't over yet. Even after the rules committee cut off all hope of releasing committed delegates, Kennedy people kept ratcheting the platform steadily to the left. Ted had brought in the tough-minded Harold Ickes, Jr. to supervise convention tactics, and quickly prevailed on planks that incorporated a $12 billion jobs program, and the guarantee of a job for every American, reproductive freedom, and the withholding of Party support from candidates who waffled on the equal rights amendment. Carter managers held fast against comprehensive health insurance and mandatory wage and price controls.

Kennedy's speech lifted all the boats. Insisting at the outset that he was there "not to argue as a candidate, but to affirm a cause," Kennedy was emotionally repositioning himself to confront a Ronald Reagan presidency. "The great adventure which our opponents offer is a voyage into the past," he offered. "Progress is our heritage, not theirs." In uncanny anticipation of the transcontinental pepper grinder through which Reagonomics would feed the wage-earners of the nation, Kennedy noted that "The poor may be out of political fashion, but they are not without human needs. The middle class may be angry, but they have not lost the dream that all Americans can advance together. . . . Let us pledge that we will never misuse unemployment, high interest rates, and human misery as false weapons against inflation. . . . The tax cut of our Republican opponents takes the name of tax reform in vain. It is a wonderfully Republican idea that would redistribute income in the wrong direction. . . .

"For me," Kennedy concluded, "a few hours ago, this campaign came to an end. For all those whose cares have been our concern, the work goes on, the cause endures, the hope still lives, and the dream shall never die."

Kennedy campaigned for Carter, if without much relish, and even that little was purchased, according to a bitter vignette in

Hamilton Jordan's memoirs, with discretionary Carter funds extracted behind closed doors by Steve Smith to defray Kennedy's campaign bills. Reagan prevailed. Joan returned to Boston, and after an interval there was a quiet divorce.

6

A decade now opened during which — except for the quadrennial speculation as to whether he would run again — Kennedy's name came up a lot less frequently in the respectable press, although the tabloids remained devoted. There was a suspicion that he was sinking bit by bit, preoccupied with booze and bimbettes. Kennedy *was* roaming widely, but somehow the opinion-makers remained oblivious to the fact that most of the working year, days and many nights, Kennedy was already engaging the Reagan administration, often all but single-handed.

"Goddamn it," Bob Shrum says now, "whatever criticism people have of this guy, just remember that in the early eighties, when everybody else was running for cover, he absolutely refused to. He stood up on stuff that was very tough to stand up on." This required for Kennedy the rethinking of alliances, the restructuring of issues frequently. He had lost his presidential bid, but he was moving now to formulate around himself something close to a shadow government.

The reversal of political tides that installed Ronald Reagan washed irreplaceable Democrats out. The House held, but many of the ablest among the younger, more liberal senators lost, so that the Senate itself passed over to the Republicans. George McGovern fell, along with Warren Magnuson and Birch Bayh and Frank Church and even John Culver. These were the stalwarts who tended to stand with Kennedy, his basis for power. Howard Baker moved up to Majority Leader, then, tapped by the White House, relinquished to Robert Dole. "That's one thing about being leader," Dole promptly acknowledged in his velvet snarl. "I don't have to let Ted Kennedy run the place."

On Labor and Human Resources, guardian of the "entitlements," Kennedy was now subject to the chairmanship of Utah conservative Orrin Hatch. "My leader," he told the press, reportedly "exploding with laughter." Kennedy emerged as Ranking Minority Member, seven Democrats versus nine Republicans. He could anticipate that little he proposed would make it out of committee.

The door blocked, Kennedy rattled the windows. Of nine committee Republicans, two tended to side with the Democrats on human services questions: education-minded Robert Stafford of Vermont and Connecticut's Lowell Weicker, by then an established maverick. Tom Rollins, who ran Kennedy's staff on the labor committee through much of the eighties, remembers the afternoon when Weicker was speechifying directly in the teeth of White House policy, while Robert Dole stood nearby, glaring. "I know what you guys are thinking," Weicker broke off to tell Dole. "You'd like to trade me for a Democrat and two draft picks."

"Forget the draft picks," Dole muttered.

While acknowledging that there was little the Democrats could do to forestall the $23 billion in cuts to social programs the Reagan administration demanded, Kennedy concentrated on keeping the programs themselves alive. Since 1933,

Democratic presidents had lobbied to weave into the books what commentators would come to refer to as the "social safety net." Starting with the Social Security and minimum wage legislation and labor union provisions enacted under the New Deal, and expanded in the rush of Lyndon Johnson's New Frontier to provide for Medicare and Medicaid as well as the breakthrough Civil and Voting Rights requirements, these sweeping and bitterly contested protections and entitlements altered profoundly the relationship between voters and their government.

Wide-ranging, costly, and replete with millions of patronage jobs and opportunities for limitless pork-barrel tradeoffs, this infrastructure of welfare remained a glory to the Left and a compounding stomachache of increasing taxes and overlapping federal regulation to the traditional Right. To politicians of every persuasion, it looked like money and influence. Among the cabinet posts, the ever-expanding Department of Health and Human Services disposed of a far bigger budget than any other bureaucracy, dwarfing even the Pentagon. Its counterpart in the Senate, the Committee on Labor and Human Resources, was well positioned to authorize and direct these colossal nationwide expenditures.

So it was not a complete surprise when Edward Kennedy decided prior to the 1980 elections to relinquish the leadership of the prestigious Judiciary Committee in return for the chairmanship of Labor and Human Resources. In any fruitful year, most of the big-ticket legislation working its way through Congress would now come directly beneath his hand. He and his sharp-eyed staffers could tinker with, define the terms, where necessary, recut provisions before they became subject to the politicizing give-and-take of routine committee debate. He could quietly scuttle anything obnoxious. Whatever got reported out, made it onto the Senate floor and came up for voting — he'd leave his fingerprints on that. When finally the House version came along, and senators had to be selected for the conference so that a reconciled bill might emerge for the president's signature, senatorial usage would mandate that the Chairman — or the Ranking Minority Member — retain the privilege of challenging such delegates as the Majority Leader selected.

Although denied the chairmanship in 1980 by the unexpected loss of the Senate to a Republican majority, as Ranking Minority Member Kennedy quickly proved himself maddeningly dangerous and inventive. With help from Stafford and Weicker Kennedy preserved a range of services, from school-lunch subsidies to the $25,000 limit on family income for students applying for college loans. He maneuvered to keep Title I education funds out of block grants to the states, resisted cuts in Social Security, made sure the low-income fuel assistance program continued, fought off the termination of the services of the Comprehensive Employment and Training Act (CETA). On the Senate floor he prevailed over Hatch's effort to gut legal assistance to the poor, which survived with two-thirds of its allocation after a 74-26 vote.

"After the '80 campaign," Kennedy recalled to me recently, "even before the inauguration, it was very, very clear to me that the focus and attention of the Reagan presidency was to undermine the basic construct of the human-services programs, which I had always thought were not to be sort of a handout but a hand up." To slow down this wrecking crew, Kennedy made his alliances where he found them. As the Ranking Democrat on Labor and Human Resources, Kennedy managed to enlist a newly elected conservative from Indiana, Dan Quayle, in pushing through the Job Training Partnership Act, which appealed to some Republicans as a replacement for

CETA. Funded at $3.9 billion, it created a mechanism through which private industry groups and local officials would provide one million job slots, train 2-3 million new workers a year.

The bill got through, Kennedy remembers, but Quayle was "basically stiffed by the White House, which urged other Republicans not to attend quorums and conference committees. Even after it passed, they weren't going to have a signing ceremony for him."

So it was wading against the tide those long Republican years. "I mean, you're talking about an administration that opposed the extension of the Voting-Rights Act," Kennedy summed it up with a toss of his mane.

Subparagraph by subparagraph, Kennedy and what diehards he could convince managed to deflect or at worst slow down the bulldozing of half a century of social engineering. This was depressing work, Rollins remembers, a matter of slapping a hold on whatever the administration was pushing, of never passing anything by unanimous consent and forcing Republican tradeoffs to keep any proposal alive. Rollins cites one "ugly, bruising" interlude during which Kennedy and his staff spent four days in a hearing room to block the appointment of the conservative lawyer Jeff Zuckerman as general counsel of the Equal Employment Opportunity Commission when Clarence Thomas was chairman. On day three the questioning got so rough Zuckerman sobbed, and in the end he went down.

Since "hearings" could not be authorized without a committee majority, Kennedy found that he could attract press and force public attention by reinventing the hearing under another rubric. This he would call the "forum." Once witnesses were alerted, Kennedy booked the Senate caucus room and excoriated the administration over the hypocrisies behind "constructive engagement" in South Africa or nation-building in Central America. This alternative format added nuclear winter to the national nightmare after the Soviet scientist Yevgeniy Velikhov and Carl Sagan testified that a nuclear exchange could blanket the stratosphere with dust and deny the planet enough sunlight for life to survive.

Within months of the inauguration Kennedy had argued against administration proposals to strip $749 billion from corporate and personal taxes through 1986. This "tree ripe with the richest plums for the wealthiest individuals and corporations" would produce "only bitter fruit for workers and middle class," Kennedy prophesied. What sort of monetary policy was this under which "Gulf and Mobil can borrow over $5 billion each in a single two-day period, but a working family cannot obtain a home mortgage even at the fantastic rate of 19 percent?" If "Ronald Reagan does not know the facts about how this recession began, then Ed Meese ought to wake him up and tell him!"

Aghast at the "jellybean economics" catching hold across Reagan-era America, Kennedy drove an amendment through which directed the administration to "take appropriate action on a voluntary basis to encourage banking or other financial institutions to exercise voluntary restraints in extending credit for the purpose of unproductive large-scale corporative takeovers." Nineteen eighty-one wasn't finished, and Kennedy was already projecting the decade's catastrophic banking failures, its looming deficit calamities.

In 1982, ignoring the traditional limitation of two major committee appointments per senator, Kennedy convinced his Republican colleagues to grant him a seat on the Armed Services Committee to add to Justice and Labor and Human Resources. Kennedy prepared to comment on — and involve himself in — a wide array of defense and foreign policy questions. "He doesn't steal credit," observed James Wieghart, the respected former D.C. bureau chief of *The New York Daily News* who handled the press for Kennedy for a time. "He just absorbs it." Kennedy was already criticizing the projected $180 billion arms buildup, the resurrection of the "discredited and extravagant B-1 bomber," additional nuclear aircraft carriers. With Armed Services credentials he continued to attack the B-1 as a "supersonic Edsel in the sky," the MX as a "missile without a mission." As for Star Wars: "We must reject the preposterous notion of a lone ranger in the sky, firing silver laser bullets and shooting missiles out of the hands of Soviet outlaws."

Kennedy spoke against the administration's dispatch of fifty-four military advisors to support the repression in El Salvador. As Reagan's first term was winding to an end, Kennedy was vociferous in his attacks against U.S. military involvement throughout Central America. His success in cutting back $21 million in aid to the Contras along with $62 million to El Salvador was telling enough by March of 1984 to alarm Rob Simmons, the CIA retiree who looked after the majority's interests as staff director for the Senate Select Committee on Intelligence.

The Agency's covert mining of Managua harbor had surfaced in the press that week, Barry Goldwater was outraged ("I've pulled Casey's nuts out of the fire on so many occasions," Goldwater exclaimed to Simmons, "I feel like such a fool"), and Simmons was especially concerned because "Teddy Kennedy was going to attack the funding" on the Senate floor. On April 19, by a vote of 84-12, Kennedy marshaled a resolution through the Republican-controlled Senate that recommended a ban on the use of U.S. funds to mine Nicaraguan waters, "a first step," Kennedy specified, "to halt President Reagan's secret war in Nicaragua." "It was the first debate on the floor of the Senate on U.S. policy in Central America," his national security assistant Greg Craig recalls, "and it would not have happened if Ted Kennedy had not single-handedly involved himself."

This, along with Representative Boland's amendments in the House, helped move along the excruciating process which led to cease-fires throughout the region. Closer senatorial attention would culminate in the Iran-Contra scandals. Despite himself, Barry Goldwater was impressed. He professed to be horrified ("oh my god, here we go again") when Kennedy first wangled his way into Armed Services, but the Massachusetts senator's attentiveness as chair of the Tactical Warfare Subcommittee to the feelings and requirements of the senior brass forced Goldwater to admit that "you are a valuable member of the committee. . . . Frankly, you have the kind of attitude that we need."

Next, Kennedy landed on the Manpower Subcommittee as the ranking Democrat, which gave him a lot of input as to the distribution of perhaps $85 billion a year of defense money. Kennedy recut his schedule to visit U.S. military installations around the world, from troop ships of the Southern command headed for equatorial waters to Lockheed's experimental "skunkworks" in California, and became a champion of enlisted troops especially. Kennedy spoke for the Marine Corps, and defended the Osprey helicopter. He gave his attention to concerns like spousal employment on bases, day care, health and education availability and pay levels — counterparts to the issues on which he was himself expert after years on the Labor Committee. "He did the nitty-gritty work," Greg Craig emphasizes. "Not high profile. You weren't going to run for president doing that stuff."

His Armed Services involvement made him a lot more credible once he began to critique the ever-swelling Reagan budget. Kennedy swung his influence behind the enhancement of conventional forces, cruise missile technology, stealth aircraft, the missile submarine armada, perfected command and control systems. Echoing JFK's non-proliferation concerns, Ted became the Senate's foremost spokesman for negotiating a bilateral nuclear freeze. He now saw clearly the connection between U.S. support for ruling elites around the world and the emergence of revolutionary challenges. "Instead of cutting off food stamps to our own people," Kennedy implored Democrats at their midterm convention in 1982, "let us cut back the feast of military aid to fatten dictatorships around the world." It wouldn't be long before old friends like Panamanian businessman Gabriel Lewis would alert Kennedy to the back-alley corruption and abuses by administration favorite Manuel Noriega, Panama's increasingly controversial strongman.

Kennedy swamped Republican businessman Ray Shamie in Massachusetts in 1982, and there were stirrings toward a 1984 presidential effort. When Kennedy and Fritz Mondale both showed up at a breakfast rally in Iowa in October 1982, Kennedy ventured that "Some people have even written in the newspaper that we're out here forming political organizations for the future.

"Well, let me tell you, Vice President Mondale and I don't like to read those stories. He doesn't like to read 'em about me, and I don't like to read 'em about him."

Before the end of that year Kennedy had already withdrawn, emphasizing in his statement that it was "very soon" to expect his children to go through such an experience again, especially since "the decision that Joan and I have made about our marriage has been painful for our children as well as ourselves." His children had been "very sophisticated" in arguing their opposition, and put the stress on all he could accomplish by persevering in the Senate.

Not that he was ready quite yet to give up twitting the possibility. His New Year's wishes, Kennedy suggested early in 1983, were "Jobs, a nuclear freeze, and Patrick changes his mind."

For all that, as early as 1985 Kennedy took himself out of consideration for the 1988 presidential race; the decision "much increased my effectiveness in the Senate," he now maintains. He cites in particular the way this decision helped "build a coalition here in favor of sanctions against South Africa. . . . My stepping back helped us override a presidential veto of the sanctions," he recalls. "When you're a presidential contender, you always get more attention around here but less credibility. When you're not, you get more credibility but less attention. That's always been the classic commentary." Regrets about abandoning his presidential aspirations? "I always felt that was more in perceptions than what I was actually doin' around here," Kennedy throws out, and changes the subject.

Truthfully, Kennedy was always relieved enough to have his *Massachusetts* reelection tucked away. The process invariably looked a lot more automatic to outsiders than it did to Kennedy. In 1988 he topped the hit list of Terry Dolan's National Conservative Political Action Committee (NCPAC), and there were those around Washington who felt that bumping Ted Kennedy would do the Right more good than enthroning Ronald Reagan. NCPAC's promotional literature projected Kennedy as Jabba the Hut, a vast, heartless monster of collectivistic appetites intent on slurping down, alive and wriggling, the plethora of tax breaks and trust fund incomes and offshore opportunities on which the propertied classes continued to depend.

Worse, shortly after his 1980 primary defeat, Kennedy started up his own political action committee, The Fund for a Democratic Majority, and it was shortly raising upwards of $500,000 a year, intended for selected senatorial candidates. This meant to alarmists on the right that, along with his overloaded domestic agenda and an increasingly grating tendency to mouth off on defense policy, Kennedy commanded a war chest. He could pick favorites and skew election results anywhere he chose. He'd booted the presidency, but with a staff which again approached one hundred he amounted to a one-man government in exile.

Virtually every White House initiative had to allow for Kennedy's demonstrated genius at laying parliamentary roadblocks or enlisting public opinion to quash the unacceptable. His talent for "marking up" a piece of legislation behind closed doors — in committee or subcommittee, in conference with House members once bills were passed — resulted again and again in legislation that fell far short of what Reagan's business-oriented advisors had hoped to pressure from Congress. Under Kennedy's untiring guardianship the reformist agenda propounded originally by FDR survived the Reagan era.

7

〜

Among well-washed Republicans, Kennedy all but blotted out the sun. Even his person threatened. Kennedy's weight, for example, went up and down by fifty or sixty pounds according to his appetites of the season or whichever election was pending. Mike Barnicle of *The Boston Globe,* an admirer all along of Kennedy's outsider militancy in the face of the "pious whores" in both parties, devoted one hilarious column to the senator's expanding corpus. "You know where he stands," Barnicle wrote in 1984. "There's a dent in the ground." Barnicle insisted that Ted sent out for "wider laurels to rest on," and that — unkindest of all — "When the Republicans talk about cutting the fat out of the budget, Kennedy takes it personally."

Periodically, Kennedy undertook a diet of "chocolate glop," forewent the extensive catered lunch, complete with an inch-thick slice of prime rib and a choice Bordeaux, which eased his midday schedule. Spokesmen blamed a weakness for ice cream for the senator's girth. But Kennedy himself, braced by a posse of reporters, waved all that away one afternoon to confess, freely, "It's the sauce, boys," before lurching toward another committee room.

How bad was Kennedy's drinking? At times, under stress, his hands trembled badly, purportedly a familial problem. Blotches disfigured the swell of his cheeks, while along his nose, where reconstructive surgery had left a kind of polyp to replace a basal cell skin cancer, there remained a dense permanent shine. Kennedy's thick, wavy hair now seemed to be silvering overnight.

A story was making the rounds that Kennedy was tippling all day, so that by afternoon he couldn't make a quorum call. Such rumors remained precisely wrong: as a point of pride Kennedy habitually turned away any serious drinking so long as the Senate was in session. He abstained entirely from New Years until his — and Washington's — birthday. When deliberations ground on through the end of the afternoon or into the evening, and all the hours of standing and hoisting himself in and out of chairs had tightened his back to the point of spasm, it made him irritable with the effort to suppress the pain and harder than ever on the overworked staff that scrambled to meet his demands. "I wish this god damned thing would end," an aide remembers overhearing Kennedy mutter. "I need a vodka."

Especially for a legislator who styled himself a champion of women's rights, Kennedy's rampages after hours kept Georgetown in delectable shock. He worked the rallies and conventions unabashedly. Although he was scrupulous about insulating policy people, regulars around the office sometimes found themselves on discreet assignments unrelated to any law. One stalwart was delegated each Christmastime to pick up identical silk scarves for good sports throughout the Republic on whom the senator periodically dropped in unannounced.

Others found themselves bird-dogging a live prospect across a crowded reception, under orders to recommend a drink in the back of the senator's limousine, or even — there were verified claims — perhaps a line of coke. Like JFK's, Ted's hands were subject to roaming quite widely, under tablecloths and between the seats on commercial flights. Enough gossip got around to keep the matrons of Washington uneasy, many fearful that Kennedy might lumber in and plant himself alongside one of *their* daughters.

Nevertheless — pace *The National Enquirer* — it remained a fact that Kennedy spent most evenings alone, settled in at McLean to sip on a weak Scotch while marking up the bales of paperwork the members of his various committee staffs competed to stuff into his notorious portmanteau, "The Bag." Something of an insomniac, Kennedy tended to work late and get up early to sit over breakfast with aides or imported experts before driving to Capitol Hill to take on his appointment schedule. He habitually worked two full shifts, offloading everything he could onto his army of staffers so he could confine himself to whatever specifically required a senator.

Kennedy flirted with exhaustion a lot of the time. Underneath, he was acutely lonely.

By announcing before he needed to that he would not go after the Democratic nomination in 1984, Kennedy made it easier to keep his distance from both wings of the party. In important particulars, conventional liberalism wasn't working. Even before 1980, for example, Kennedy's views had hardened as to what might produce effective law enforcement in America. He would work closely with Strom Thurmond to produce a crime control bill with bail reform, harsher sentencing, and even preventive detention, the prospects of which particularly horrified the American Civil Liberties Union. Kennedy put in time to protect these accommodations with the conservatives. After an unusually tough exchange with Thurmond during a Labor Committee embroilment, Kennedy joined the crusty South Carolinian for the walk to a Judiciary Committee meeting. "C'mon Strom," he reportedly reassured the old man, slapping a hand over his shoulder, "let's go upstairs and I'll give you a few judges."

Once Reagan was reelected, Kennedy delivered a landmark speech at Hofstra University in which he proclaimed that Democrats cannot "cede to the other side issues like economic growth and America's standing in the world." There was "a difference between being a party that cares about labor and being a labor party . . . a party that cares about women and being a women's party. We can and we must be a party that cares about minorities without becoming a minority party. We are citizens first and constituencies second."

In short order Kennedy hosted Ronald Reagan at a fundraiser at the Kennedy Center and endorsed the line-item veto to bring the budget under control. While continuing to maintain that supply-side economics "should have been left on the back of the cocktail napkin on which it was first worked out ten years ago," Kennedy broke with many of the Democrats to back the Gramm-Rudman-Hollings amendment. He called the budget process "a shambles," and admitted that "Congress is not only not part of the solution, it is definitely part of the problem."

All this was further and further from tax and spend. "You know, I liked you a lot better before I moved to the right," Kennedy chided Orrin Hatch after Orrin jibbed him a good one in debate. The prim Utah conservative couldn't help but respond at times to Kennedy's great heart and parliamentary legerdemain. He viewed Kennedy's antics around town as ripe for upgrading. "I admire him so much," Hatch conceded as early as 1982. "I'm just going to send the Mormon missionaries to him to straighten out the rest of his life." Kennedy was about to hornswoggle Labor and Human Resources into submitting an overall domestic budget $8 billion above the administration's request as well as doubling the Pell Grant money to underwrite college tuitions.

Kennedy had already discovered that Hatch's conservative imprimatur lent just enough convincing spin to legislation to give it a solid chance, and he kept looking for opportunities to support his chairman. The pair teamed up to ram through a bill to permit U.S. pharmaceutical companies to sell their product abroad before it cleared American testing requirements (biotechnology was booming in Massachusetts). They kicked up AIDS funding together, cosponsored bills on mental health, Alzheimer's research and religious freedom, joined efforts to deal with welfare dependency and a law to ban the use of lie detectors by private employers. "He's knocked a lot of rough edges off me," Hatch conceded, "and for that I'm grateful. Also, he's a first-class legislator, and whenever we work together I think we can accomplish just about anything." Some people think a bill with both their names on it, Hatch joked, "means one of us hasn't read it." Reactions around the Senate were far less infatuated. "I'm gettin' damned tired of votin' on all that Kennedy-Hatch legislation goin' through," Jesse Helms was overheard to remark.

In 1986 the Democrats recaptured the Senate. Nine of the eleven incoming freshmen Democrats got money and campaign guidance from Kennedy's Fund for a Democratic

Majority. Kennedy assumed the chairmanship of Labor and Human Resources. "When we took the Senate back he was transformed, a new man," Tom Rollins recollects. "He worked like an animal. He called me immediately and brought us up to Hyannis Port. We could not overpaper him. Nobody ever wrote a memo he thought was too long. Everything came back with his handwriting all over it. Until then what we had mostly been doing was trying to stop legislation the administration wanted, throwing as much sand in the machinery as possible.

"From then on we had a program, timetables, he managed that operation very tightly." A lot of Kennedy legislation now made it out of committee; much passed the Senate. Of this, a good deal couldn't survive the conference proceedings, and whatever got that far was likely to confront a White House veto. But important hearings, vital drafting and the accumulation of support among the colleagues prepared the way for a great deal of success once Reagan stepped down. Kennedy's popularity on both sides of the aisle was now an enduring catalyst. "If you want to find Ted Kennedy," suggested his regular drinking buddy Christopher Dodd of Connecticut, "listen for the laughter." A close aide remarks that once freshman colleagues recognized that Kennedy was not a "raving liberal lefty they tended to gravitate to him, they found his hearty Irishness attractive, compared with the standard blow-dried Republicans."

As good a case in point as any would be Kennedy's jostling, affectionate relationship with Alan Simpson, the hard-right Wyoming conservative Republican who came to Washington in 1978, like other provincial lawyers, hell-bent on forestalling the giveaway socialism Kennedy supposedly represented. Simpson's longtime advisor Dick Day has remarked that the politics of immigration is "compounded out of equal parts emotion, racism, guilt, and fear"; immigrants are not a factor in Wyoming, so Simpson was less than overjoyed to find himself drafted onto a presidential commission with Kennedy to recut immigration policy. After 1980 Simpson chaired the immigration subcommittee within the Justice Committee, with Kennedy as ranking Democrat. Together, they pieced out the 1987 Simpson-Mazolli Act (illegal immigration), along with the 1990 Kennedy-Simpson Act (legal immigration). Much amounted to a redrafting of legislation Kennedy himself had authored twenty-four years earlier.

Jerry Tinker, who directed the immigration shop for Kennedy, remembered the pair during quorum calls. "They had totally opposite senses of humor," Tinker observes. "Simpson's material tended to be Western, anecdotal, 'very rich' in flavor. Kennedy is more of a mime, a story teller. At quiet moments Simpson would sidle over in his lanky way, and kind of lean toward Kennedy, and say, 'Ted, have you heard this one?' Then he would tell some ribald classic, and Kennedy with his Irish laughter would bring the rafters down. I remember once Bobby Byrd, who is something of a stickler for decorum, came over and tried to hush them up."

For some years Kennedy and Simpson enjoyed a weekly few minutes of adversarial debate on a show called "Face-off" on the Mutual Broadcasting Network, with each carping away according to partisan dogma. This kind of ritual may satisfy the true believers, but it is a long way from life around the cloakroom of the Senate.

Not everything was reconcilable. After 1981, with White House encouragement, the largely Republican-appointed Supreme Court was trimming back civil rights interpretation. When, in

1982, the landmark Voting Rights Act of 1965 was slated to expire, the word came out of the Justice Department that it was the administration's preference that the law not be renewed. Kennedy moved in vigorously, brought Robert Dole around an inch at a time, and in the end rallied a coalition which pushed the renewal through, with provisions to override a Supreme Court decision that otherwise would have undercut it.

In 1984 the Supreme Court in the Grove City Case had ruled that Title 6 of the 1964 Education Act, which prohibited the federal government from funding educational institutions which discriminated by race, applied only to that *program* in the institution which discriminated, not to the institution overall. Kennedy promptly orchestrated passage of the Civil Rights Restoration Act to reaffirm the law's intent, and got it enacted over a presidential veto. Supported by Republican moderates, Kennedy installed some teeth in the Fair Housing Amendments Acts of 1988. He directed the passage of the Americans with Disabilities Act in 1990, working out the details with John Sununu and Attorney General Thornburgh.

The Supreme Court was still pecking away at civil rights legislation, especially where it impacted employment discrimination. The head of Kennedy's staff at the Justice Committee, Jeff Blattner, now found his boss "energetic, focused, and relentless," dug in and determined enough to break a Republican filibuster with a cloture vote, "and in the end he prevailed." Under mounting bipartisan pressure from moderates like John Danforth of Missouri, George Bush did not again veto the Civil Rights Act of 1990–91.

Without question Kennedy's bloodiest and most gratifying battle throughout the Reagan years was the confirmation donnybrook over the Supreme Court nomination of Robert Bork. With his Silenus goatee and bulging, impudent eyes, Robert Bork came over as a disheveled escapee from some subterranean think tank. Bork had the resume — law professor at Yale, important government posts, the federal bench — and at the outset nobody expected a tussle. But Kennedy hadn't forgotten that it was Bork, as Solicitor General, who contravened the agreement Kennedy himself had negotiated with the Nixon White House and — after Elliot Richardson and William Ruckleshaus refused — fired Watergate special prosecutor Archibald Cox.

Kennedy set his staff to digging, and what they unearthed confirmed his misgivings. On the day in 1987 that Reagan formally nominated Bork, Kennedy was thoroughly primed. "Robert Bork's America," he prophesied in a floor speech, "is a land in which women would be forced into back-alley abortions, blacks would sit at segregated lunch counters, rogue police could break down citizen's doors in midnight raids, schoolchildren could not be taught about evolution, writers and artists could be censored at the whim of government and the doors of the federal courts would be shut on the fingers of millions of citizens. . . ."

Crafted by Carey Parker, this speech roused overnight apprehension on the Left, and anger and resentment across the Right. It was undoubtedly overdrawn, but behind each charge Kennedy's researchers had something. In fact the strategy governing the speech, Jeff Blattner will concede, "was to alert the Senate and the country immediately to the enormous issues at stake and, in effect, to freeze senators who might otherwise have made some comment favorable to the nomination without being fully informed about Judge Bork's record and views."

Bork's opinions on central issues — voting rights, women's rights (especially Roe versus Wade), and restrictive covenants — while in some cases expressed many years earlier — "were not consonant with the constitution and equal justice under law." Kennedy mobilized his interest-group networks nationwide and talked with a number of swing senators of both parties. He coordinated closely with committee chairman Joe Biden, as well as with Allen Cranston and Howard Metzenbaum. He got Joe Lowery of the Southern Christian Leadership Conference to whip up black preachers across the country.

"There wasn't any deal-making," Blattner insists. "It was just flat-out political combat, no quarter given or taken, no horse-trading or logrolling." Robert Bork himself, increasingly indignant and unappealing, went on too long beneath the committee lights, and frequently in the wrong direction. Under Kennedy's uncompromising stage management the pressure built session by session, and in the end Bork lost, and resoundingly.

Miffed after losing Bork, managers around the White House were touchy about Kennedy's propensity to interfere with, personalize, situations overseas. He sent an adventure-loving staff man, Gare Smith, to trouble spots from Western Sahara to the backlands of Burma to dodge bullets and meet with pro-democracy activists and bring back dispassionate appraisals. A series of "forums" Kennedy convened on violence in Central America brought to Washington's attention a number of witnesses from the region, including several Miskito Indian spokesmen. Their culture was already being decimated by raids from the Sandinista army. When Daniel Ortega came to the U.N., Kennedy set up a secret six-hour meeting between the Indian leader Brooklyn Riviera and Ortega which led to a deal according to which the CIA was forced to stop instigating the Indians to attack the Sandinista regulars. Ortega too backed off, and the Miskitos soon recovered a measure of security and sovereignty in their homelands on the Atlantic coast.

Kennedy tried to reverse the polarization in El Salvador by lining up enough votes around the Senate to cut military support for the conservative government in half while establishing a close personal friendship with Jose Napolean Duarte, the gutsy Christian Democrat who represented the Salvadorans' sole alternative to the death-squad politics of Roberto d'Aubuisson. Duarte was a regular dinner guest in McLean on his periodic trips to Washington, and when the embattled Salvadoran president showed up at Walter Reed for cancer treatments Kennedy made it a point to visit him at his bedside. "In hospital situations, where he's meeting people, touching people, there's no one like him," Greg Craig would notice. "He doesn't intrude. He's gentle. But he's *there.*"

By 1987, once Panama began unraveling, Kennedy was watching closely. Most of the businessmen in Panama's reformist Civic Crusade were contacts of long standing, and Kennedy was quick, as charges of maladministration and drug running began to surface against Manuel Noriega, to put forward legislation which led to economic sanctions against the Noriega government as well as empowering a fact-finding group. Republican senators like Jesse Helms and Alphonse D'Amato were particularly incensed with Noriega, and Kennedy swiftly harnessed their irritation to keep the Senate, Craig recalls, "way out ahead of the administration."

Yet when the Bush administration launched Operation Just Cause in December of 1989, Kennedy denounced the incursion. "The feel-good invasion of Panama does not feel so good anymore," he announced, finding "nothing in the public record that justifies the invasion." He feared "the outcry against the invasion" had "significantly boosted the prospects of the

Sandinistas in the Nicaraguan elections that will take place next month."

Here, as with Desert Storm two years afterward, Kennedy made clear his dislike of military intervention. Better to try and compel real reform from within than reshuffle the principals. Greg Craig didn't agree in either situation, but advisors must advise, not decide. Kennedy preferred letting sanctions run their course.

He felt the successes of sanctions in Poland and South Africa pointed up their effectiveness. South Africa in particular — there, Kennedy had a vested emotional interest. In October of 1984, when something fast approaching a race war was rising in the Transvaal, Kennedy had a lunch with Episcopal Archbishop Desmond Tutu and Alan Boesak, both revered black leaders then attempting to create the multiracial United Democratic Front. Kennedy asked what he could do to help. Visit South Africa, they suggested.

A few weeks later Tutu won the Nobel Peace Prize. The trip was delayed for over a year. "I had always been somewhat re-luctant to go down there," Kennedy says now, "because I thought my brother Bob's trip [in June of 1966] had been such a powerful visit, with so much substance and symbolism, sort of like a bell that was continuing to ring. I didn't want to interfere with the chimes. But they were very persuasive."

Kennedy's trip in January of 1985 was exhausting and dan-gerous. His arrival in South Africa was greeted by a demonstration of angry blacks, foot soldiers for the militant anti-white radicals of AZAPO abetted by the white South African police. Ignoring the government's advice, Kennedy passed the night in Tutu's modest bungalow in Soweto. He was reportedly the first white to sleep in the tortured township. "Staying there, sleeping in the bed, seeing the Nobel Prize right next to the bed. . . ." Kennedy has to chuckle, hollowly. "He had the choir of his church come over. They sang songs. Soft songs. To put me to sleep. They just sang in the living room. I knew he was as tired as I was. He said: 'You'll sleep, I'll show you how to sleep.' You know, at first you say, my God, there's singing out there. But you know, it sort of rocks you to sleep. . . ."

Kennedy got back determined to highlight the problem. He gave a dinner party to which he invited the chairman of the Foreign Relations Committee, Richard Lugar, along with Nancy Kassebaum, the chair of the subcommittee on African affairs. Also at the table were the respected ex-president of Australia Malcolm Fraser and the former Nigerian president Obassanjo. Their inquiry and recommendations regarding South Africa would supply the blueprint for the Kennedy-Weicker bill. Committee by committee, formally and informally, the Kennedy-Weicker "tag-team" worked colleagues on both sides of the aisle and in the end drove through a bill which initially cut off investment in South Africa until the repression was lifted. The sanction bill went through after two years to face the predictable Reagan veto, which the Senate overruled by eleven votes. South Africa would evolve.

Kennedy inherited the prerogative — at least, he assumed he did — to pursue an independent foreign policy vis-à-vis the Soviet Union. "My brothers had a relationship with Dobrynin which went back with them, and went back with me . . . I started to visit the Soviet Union in 1974." There was a long meeting then and in 1978 with Brezhnev. Each time Kennedy traveled to Moscow, conditions of his visit were negotiated in advance — so many refuseniks to receive exit visas, so much time on radio or television. "I remember one speech at the University of Moscow, where they said I could talk to the whole school. But then they gave me a very small hall. They had those kinds of little dances."

Everything changed when Gorbachev took over in 1985. Kennedy found the new General Secretary "robust, expansive, responsive to questions. Challenging, self-confident — certainly an entirely different kind of Soviet leader than we'd met at other times." He'd known Foreign Secretary Eduard Shevardnadze since 1978. Furthermore, as a member of the Senate Arms Control Delegation, Kennedy sat in on meetings two or three times a year with Soviet experts like V. V. Alexandrov and Velikhov. The Russians remained alarmed at the prospect of a "Nuclear Winter" in the event of an atomic exchange. Even after he formally left the senator's employ, Kennedy's key aide during the later seventies, Dr. Larry Horowitz, went back and forth to keep himself abreast of the debate at meetings, there were early forums, and over the Reagan years Kennedy's office began to function for the Soviets as a back-channel to American politics.

When, toward the end of Reagan's second term, the Soviets thought seriously about scrapping their intermediate-range ballistic missiles, they went to Kennedy first, who got the word to the administration's senior arms negotiator, Max Kampelman. Kennedy and his experts sat in on a number of the exchanges, and when the Intermediate-Range Nuclear Force missile treaty was signed in 1988 Secretary of State George Shultz acknowledged the senator's contribution.

By 1990 *Pravda* was headlining the greeting Soviet President Gorbachev had extended to his "old friend, Edward Kennedy." The senator was in Moscow to plead for Soviet restraint in Lithuania and underline to the Russians that the United States was not very likely to negotiate away its command of the seas. Yet at the same time, Kennedy was interested in exploring with the Soviets ways to verify the location of underwater nuclear weaponry. Kennedy hoped to bring back *something* with which to cajole the Bush administration into dealing with sea power during the ongoing disarmament negotiations.

As with domestic matters, Kennedy kept his experts and intermediaries probing whatever opportunies he spotted, stocking him with background information and sounding out every possibility. As a situation ripened — in Central America, in South Africa and China, in the Soviet Union — Kennedy would intervene personally, prodding both Congress and often enough a sluggish administration into formulations and results. All this was normally a responsibility of the president. But Kenedy saw nothing in the Constitution to prevent him from helping the president along.

8

The administration sometimes welcomed a hand from Kennedy, especially on the sly. Still, once he got re-elected in Massachusetts and returned to the Senate in 1988, Kennedy had picked up so much legislative momentum, along with an enhanced majority, that key Republicans started looking at each other. "Behind the scenes we've become good friends," Orrin Hatch told one reporter. "But I've found he's tough in the clinches." To another reporter Hatch confessed that, in a fight over principle, Kennedy "will murder you, he'll roll right over you. . . . He'll trample you in the ground and then he'll grind his heel in you." Still, Orrin couldn't help liking Ted.

On issues like the bill prohibiting plant closings without advance notice to workers and freedom of choice Kennedy was streamrolling the debate, and not in a direction even indulgent Republicans were pleased to go. "You can talk to Ted, you can reason with him, you can bargain with him," New Hampshire's hard-nosed Warren Rudman conceded. "Sure he's an inflexible liberal — if he's got the votes. If he doesn't, he'll deal. He's a pragmatist, he's damned effective. He's a force to be reckoned with."

Nick Littlefield came on as staff director of Kennedy's Labor committee, and virtually by the day things started to open up. The Bush administration "holds office but doesn't know what to do with it," Kennedy said in March of 1989. He was thinking aloud. Here was a vacuum to be filled. Two years later the 101st Congress turned out to have been the most productive generator of remedial social legislation since Lyndon Johnson's heyday. Of sixty-three proposals put forward by the Senate's Democratic Policy Committee, fifty-seven became law, with half, 28, originating in Kennedy's Labor Committee. They included the 1990 Child Care Act and the National and Community Services Act, and expanded Head Start, the vast, groundbreaking Americans with Disabilities Act, the McKinney Homeless Assistance Act, the Perkins Vocational Education Program, the Excellence in Math and Science Act, the National Health Service Corps, the Ryan-White AIDS Care Act, and on and on down to the raising of the minimum wage and the reauthorization of the National Endowment Act without the "content restrictions" for which the likes of Jesse Helms were fulminating.

After 1990, pummeled worse every month by Republican ideologues and worried about reelection, Bush began to bring down a series of vetoes on innovations like the Family Leave Bill and even the reauthorization of the Kennedy-initiated National Institutes of Health, while marshaling Senate Republicans to block the elementary and secondary school reform proposals and the Striker Replacement Bill. These ideas were suspended for the moment, but they were out there now in public debate, and they would all soon become, as Littlefield notes, "major themes of the Clinton campaign," and help

Clinton "focus attention on the do-nothing quality of the Bush administration in the domestic area."

Perhaps it was accidental that, just as Edward Kennedy was taking on unimagined legislative velocity, another fusillade of books and articles came in, concentrated on his private life. Most wounding — and thorough — was undoubtedly Michael Kelly's long piece in GQ in February of 1990. Kelly presented an album of relentlessly candid shots of an uncouth and bibulous fraternity roustabout, the sort of "Regency rake" prefigured in Hogarth. This rude, besotted figure seemed most of the time at sport with nubile lobbyists under tables in well-appointed restaurants or toppled across some enthusiast in the well of a speedboat off Saint Tropez.

Many of the liveliest stories featured horseplay with Chris Dodd. There was the time the two well-lubricated senators supposedly grabbed up the woman who was serving them for a terrifying round of "waitress toss," or dueled with gladiolus stalks, or executed the Mexican hat dance on pictures of themselves they plucked from cafe walls. Another account finds Dodd, naked along with a pair of cheerful nudettes, sneaking across the back lawn at McLean to rap on Kennedy's window, flaunting a bottle of champagne and demanding a Jacuzzi, totally astonishing Kennedy's bed partner of the evening.

Christopher Dodd had replaced to a certain extent the accommodating Joey Gargan, who during the earlier decades invariably cleared his schedule for a spree with cousin Ted. But life got bumpier for the ingenuous Gargan, he disliked Kennedy's stand on abortion, and after he contributed to Leo Damore's rakeover of Chappaquiddick (*Senatorial Privilege,* 1988) the cousins would keep their distance. The news break in

Damore's book, purportedly based on Gargan's confession, alleged that Ted had tried to pressure Joey into filing a false accident report, according to which *Joey* was at the wheel.

Gargan never went public with the charge directly, and, although a right-wing publisher did print the book in 1988, the allegation served finally to further degrade everyone involved.

Although Kennedy was undoubtedly on the prowl, and did lapse sometimes into "binge drinking," everybody around him insists that more and more Kennedy's free moments centered on relationships with "substantive, fortyish women." His taste still ran to long-stemmed blondes, in most cases accomplished, sweet-tempered ladies he took quite seriously for a season or two and courted with such energy that they were dazzled and permanently intrigued. A number would remain friends. The list would run over the course of the eighties from Countess Lana Campbell to Susan Saint James to Terry Muilenberg and, toward the end, Dragana Lickle, with aesthetes like Lacey Neuhaus Dorn presiding at intimate dinner parties at McLean attended by a few select couples; Tennessee Senator Jim Sasser and his wife were regulars. Kennedy dated an earnest senior aide from the Labor Committee for a time, and there was one extravagantly endowed flight attendant who disappeared with Kennedy on getaways over several seasons, a playful, good-natured counterpoint throughout a number of relationships.

Important romances soon took on a moonlight-and-roses quality, but inevitably the moment came when commitment loomed. Kennedy would pull shy and break things off. "I just couldn't bear to try again at marriage and have everything come apart on me again," he told a close friend.

———

One day in 1987 Kennedy invited Bob Shrum to dinner. "I went out there thinking it would be the usual thing," Shrum recalls. "There would be seven or eight people, and we'd have dinner, and sit around and talk afterwards.

"But there were just the two of us. We had this long dinner, and I couldn't figure out what the heck was going on. And afterwards he said, 'Let's go in the library and have a drink.'

"So we did. And then he looked at me suddenly, and he said, 'I think you ought to get married.' I had been going out for some time at that point with Mary Louise. 'You've fallen in love,' Ted told me. 'I can tell. All your friends can tell. It would be very good for you. It's a wonderful thing to find someone.'

"Kennedy is not a person who *ever* indulges in couch conversation, and I was so taken aback that I could hardly speak. He meant it, clearly, and I almost found it wistful. Because what he was saying, at least to me, was that he wished he could find the same thing. My wife and I sometimes joke that Ted Kennedy was our marriage counselor."

So there were contradictory tensions, the frustrations of too much bachelorhood. Accordingly, once in a while, Kennedy tended to pull the cork and let the demons erupt. Too many blue suits sometimes, too many months straight of standing with his arms out while security people strapped on the kevlar vest or aides writhed as Kennedy's perspiring driver jerked in and out of traffic to overtake the last shuttle departing National. Alcohol made him real to himself for a couple of hours, and that was frequently enough.

They'd deal with breakage afterward. Kennedy's irreplaceable staff aide Melody Miller, who's watched one damage control prodigy after another since Chappaquiddick, laughs about the evening she boosted Kennedy into his overcoat the night before a recess with the reminder, "Now, remember about telephoto lenses. They come *this long,* and they can pick things up for *miles."*

It requires Melody's tact — along with her years in service — to carry that off. References to Kennedy's indulgences can chill the air, bring on the snittiness nobody likes to deal with. "If that's what we're going to talk about," Kennedy jibbed David Burke, generations of advisors ago, one afternoon when Burke had the temerity to refer to one of Kennedy's wilder weekends, "why don't I lie down here on the couch? How much do you get for your services, doctor? Is it still $75 an hour?" Ted Kennedy reportedly cut off John Culver for four years for lecturing him about alcoholism.

Most staff members saw little or nothing of Kennedy when he was out and roistering. But mention his smoking days, and many still wrinkle their noses. As early as the sixties, Kennedy liked to puff on a little Filipino cigar when riding in a car or after a meal. Then, toward the end of the seventies, he took a liking to big, heavy Davidoffs, imported from Geneva. Alan Simpson, who hated the dry, acrid smoke, silently bore with Kennedy for several weeks when they were drafting the new immigration laws. One day Kennedy arrived, cigar in hand. "Ted," Simpson told him, "you can bring anyone, or anything, or any idea into this office. But you can't bring that cigar."

By the later eighties Steve Smith was dying of lung cancer. The role of Smith inside that generation of Kennedys could take a while to explain. He had a function among his in-laws that kept him involved as crisis manager and controller extraordinaire, mother hen and trigger-tempered martinet. Himself the scion of a substantial New York shipping fortune, Smith had the fine-boned boyish demeanor along with the Cafe-

Society self-assurance that tended at close quarters to elude his surviving in-laws. I remember well, months before Bobby died, standing next to him at the bottom of a slalom course in New Hampshire watching Smith carve smooth, economical turns, another order of athlete from the ragtag of Kennedys slamming between the flags. "He could still miss a gate!" Bobby turned to me and all but hissed, between a curse and a prayer.

But Smith hadn't missed. He rarely missed. By financial primogeniture Smith had fallen heir to the management of the Ambassador's estate. Several times I visited him in the warren of offices in the Pan Am building from which he tracked the investments of Joseph P. Kennedy, Inc. Once — the door was open — I overheard a tirade as the invoice for a fur coat in California came across his desk. He seemed quite accessible — he confided in me on one occasion as to his own smothered political ambitions, forever kept on hold as one after the other of the brothers went on to press for higher office. He could be devastatingly testy — I asked him once why it took him so long to make his way back to Cape Cod from Majorca, where he was vacationing, the week after Chappaquiddick; I feared for several bitter seconds that he intended to fly straight over his desk and rip open my throat.

Throughout Smith's tenure the Joseph P. Kennedy holdings had tended to bog down in real estate, especially the Merchandise Marts. But lucky or otherwise, Smith continued to carry authority. He tempered with responsibility. He remained uncharacteristically indulgent with timorous, dedicated Lem Billings, Jack's roommate-for-life and for many years a fixture around the Pan Am suite. Capital preservation remained primary. When Ted's presidential move floundered, who else but Steve could reach in and turn his water off?

The news that Steve was terminal sent a paralyzing *frisson* through the Kennedy family. For Ted in particular this feisty, chain-smoking brother-in-law had become like a surviving brother. The two were close enough to accommodate almost anything in each other, but one day — Steve was terribly weakened — he beckoned Kennedy closer. The senator had already developed an ominous, rasping cough. "Teddy," he all but whispered, "you should stop smoking."

When Kennedy next visited Smith in his hospital bed he was largely comatose. Kennedy wanted to tell him that the family had decided to name the new wing of the Kennedy Library after Steve, but he would never be certain Smith understood. In November of 1989 Kennedy introduced an anti-smoking bill. He regretted that he had started smoking cigars, he testified. Now he would try and stop. He did stop, and before long his hack abated.

Steve's death in 1990 left Kennedy more bereft than ever. Mourners at Steve's funeral watched Kennedy get up and endeavor to deliver the eulogy. After breaking down again and again Kennedy signaled to his son Patrick to come to the pulpit and take over for him. Robert, Jr. was about to step forward when Kennedy was able to pull himself together enough to get through what he had. To one Kennedy veteran it was like watching Ted crumpled in the washroom in Los Angeles the night Bobby died. He seemed utterly frozen with pain, lost, almost catatonic.

9

More, certainly, than alcohol, it's important to factor in Steve Smith's death to comprehend properly the "Palm Beach incident," the publicity extravaganza and ordeal by innuendo that threatened for some months to extinguish Kennedy's career. Like the Chappaquiddick cookout, Good Friday that fateful Easter weekend of 1991 at Palm Beach started out as a deferred wake, the chance to come to terms with the anguish of a loss.

"And we were visiting in the patio after dinner," Kennedy himself would testify months afterward, "and the conversation was a very emotional conversation, a very difficult one. Brought back a lot of very special memories to me, particularly with the loss of Steve, who really was a brother to me and to the other members of the family. And I found at the end of that conversation that I was not able to think about sleeping. It was a very draining conversation. . . . So we left that place, and we went to, out. We went to Au Bar's. I wish I'd gone for a long walk on the beach instead."

Florida changes the lighting. La Guerida, the crumbling Kennedy vacation compound on North Ocean Boulevard, has serviced four generations of off-duty family by now. This is the tile-roofed Mizner hacienda Joe picked up at depression prices to accommodate the vacation needs of Jimmy Roosevelt and Clare and Henry Luce and the appreciative Cardinal Spellman. Joe had his stroke on a golf course near this house. Robert Kennedy's son David would overdose in a motel nearby on a visit to his grandmother. Here, in a deck chair on the back lawn, Jack Kennedy marked up the galleys of *Profiles in Courage* while his back mended in 1957. He picked his cabinet members here, and the night he died some of his tony Republican neighbors reportedly celebrated his assassination at "many large parties," toasting Lee Harvey Oswald and embracing this turn of events as "wonderful news."

So Palm Beach remained at once a temptation and a bed of thorns. With Rose too enfeebled to bear up through the plane trip south any more, groups of her descendants booked time at the increasingly neglected old fortress for weekends and holidays; this helped keep vacation costs reasonable. Ever since the fifties the holdings of the Kennedys have remained surprisingly stagnant, much of their assessed value — the figure usually released runs in the $400-600 million range — tied up around Chicago. Recently, a series of poorly timed speculations by a New York investment maven bit deeper into capital. Joe's children still indulge themselves with a lavish hand, but even during Steve Smith's tenure the grandchildren were on notice.

Palm Beach was also a venue for discharging more intimate family responsibilities. From time to time her keepers would convey the lobotomized Rosemary from the desolate and now — except for her — deserted Catholic boarding school in

Wisconsin where she has been grumbling through her decades so she could spend a couple of days in the sun with whichever of the siblings could make it down. Well into her seventies now, Rosemary likes to take a drink. But drinking makes her morose, depression seems to trigger some subcategory of Tourette's syndrome, and as she wanders off muttering four-letter imprecations Rosemary's brother and sisters are left to shrug their shoulders and regard one another.

Thus, Palm Beach for the Kennedys remains beset with phantoms. Ted and his younger son Patrick arrived that Easter of 1991 at the invitation of his sister Jean, who had assembled a floating party of perhaps ten including her grown children Willy and Amanda and the retired FBI agent and JFK bodyguard William Barry and his son. The agenda was free-form. The seniors would talk, mostly, which gave the younger people opportunity to group off and experiment with the night life.

Palm Beach at night has maintained its reputation through much of the century — a string of watering holes where exhausted money meets avid, heartless climbers. Too agitated to think about sleeping after hours of reminiscences, Edward Kennedy had "noticed both Patrick and my nephew Will go by the glass windows which are just adjacent to the patio" of the Palm Beach estate, "and I opened the door and called for Will and Patrick and they answered. And I asked them whether they wanted to go out — I needed to talk to Patrick or to William — and they said yes they would."

Summoned by the patriarch, the younger men accompanied Ted to the hotspot of the season just then, Au Bar, on Royal Poinciana Way. It has been said that Kennedy is like a shark who presses on day and night to keep from drowning in a sea of memories. But it is also still true that he appreciates a party.

As *Boston Globe* reporter Jack Farrell discovered reading pretrial depositions, the evening in question "was not the first night that week the boys — including Ted — had gone to Au Bar and picked up girls and brought them home."

There remains some confusion about the chronology here — Willy Smith's sister Amanda would claim that he picked her up along with some friends at another boîte, Lulu's, at two that morning — but there is no question that during the early hours Kennedy and his party settled in around an Au Bar table. Already confronting tax troubles, the club was written up locally as "a Eurotrash kind of place." In business since November, its opening night turnout had included, according to the *Palm Beach Post,* "royalty, a few nonviolent felons, gigolos (one reportedly has his chest hair dyed), society princesses, plus Senator Ted Kennedy (he'll spend Christmas in Hawaii) and a less noticed Senator Christopher Dodd."

That early Saturday morning before Easter Kennedy and his party sat quietly, overshadowed by the return of Ivana Trump, in town for the polo matches. Patrick — who overcame a severe cocaine problem by spending a summer during the mid-eighties in Spofford Hall, the drug and alcohol rehabilitation center outside Keene, New Hampshire — was careful to confine himself to a couple of ginger ales. A tall, low-keyed, susceptible youngster with scrupulously parted auburn hair and the eyes of a frightened witness, still subject to perilous asthma attacks, Patrick had lived on at home in McLean when his mother relocated to Boston, and he and his father had become particularly close and mutually accepting. Kennedy campaigned when Patrick ran for the Rhode Island legislature in 1988 ("What a comedown!" the senator had exclaimed to a by-stander. "Eight years ago I was a presidential contender, and here I am pushing doorbells in Providence."), and stood by apprehensively while his son had a tumor removed from his spine.

"He's my life," Patrick told one interviewer, explaining why he was founding his own political career. He "wanted to follow in my father's footsteps, but leave my own tracks behind." His father had always "asked my opinion on issues he was working on. That's how I was able to cope with the fact that his work was very intrusive in our lives. I could accept it without being resentful."

People drift into conversation easily at a singles club, and not very long after they arrived Patrick found himself bantering with a local woman named Anne Mercer, who quickly moved over to attach herself to the Kennedy party accompanied by *her* friend, the twenty-nine-year-old divorcée Patricia Bowman. The mood was withdrawn among the Kennedys, not to say depressed. "Patrick looked like he was having a terrible time," Anne would note afterward, "and I said to him, jokingly, 'you look like you're having a great time,' and Senator Kennedy said to me, 'Who are you to say anything?'"

Throughout Kennedy's adult life, periodically, the need becomes urgent for a few hours of societal bottom-feeding. Rose Kennedy had suffered because the nice people of Boston never invited her over, and Jack Kennedy quipped that even after he left the presidency he still wouldn't be eligible for Boston's better clubs.

Ted Kennedy carried his bruises, and from time to time they showed. "I suppose you're finding them a lot more . . . more *interesting* than we ever were," he responded one night when I ran into him in the lobby of the Sheraton Ritz. His face was flushed with whiskey and the exertion of addressing a conference room of Catholic priests. I'd been at work for years on a transgenerational history of the Mellon family. Descendants of the Mellons obviously had a certain authenticity in Ted's eyes compared with the Kennedys, whose claim to aristocracy — even royalty — originated for the most part in some press agent's trunk of special effects.

This produced an awkwardness at times with peers, a sense of compounding social strain. There was a relief in luxuriating among commoner people, in harvesting the devotion of cast-offs and upmarket Lumpen which tended to congregate in bideawees like Au Bar while the world was sleeping. Yet exposure risked rejection sometimes, the disappointments of lèse-majesté. When one went slumming, the least one might count on was a few moments of unalloyed adoration.

Around three, his back aching and his feelings bruised, Edward Kennedy, Patrick, and somebody Patrick had attracted, a waitress named Michele Cassone, decided to abandon the overcrowded club and head back to La Guerida. Willy Smith by then was dancing with Patricia Bowman, and they would return separately.

Back at the mansion Cassone remembers sitting on an esplanade above the crashing of the surf and talking. They discussed "big families and scuba diving," she revealed afterward, although most of the time "it was Senator Kennedy holding court." At one point a tall, naked woman with slicked-back hair stalked through the shadows along the sand and into the ocean.

Soon afterward the young people excused themselves. A couple of minutes before four, Michele Cassone would recall, while she and Patrick were "cuddling" in one of the downstairs rooms, Patrick's father appeared in what was apparently his nightshirt. He was "just there with a weird look on his face," Michele insists. "I was weirded out."

"I'm out of here," Michele Cassone proclaimed. Patrick walked her to her car. "Does your father embarrass you?" Michele demanded of Patrick. It was a moonlit, semitropical night on which Kennedy obviously felt haunted, and out of date. Meanwhile, on a nearby stage, Patricia Bowman and William Kennedy Smith were playing out the *pas de deux* that ultimately lit up a hundred million television screens.

Patrick Kennedy would allude to having run into Patricia Bowman while she was in and out of the mansion a few times, before Anne Mercer appeared to drive her home. Patricia had unnerved Willy, who expressed his relief that he had "pulled out" in time and conveyed to Patrick his apprehension that she was the sort of person who "comes to your house, who is insisting on finding out whether he is a Kennedy or not." She was "sort of a fatal attraction," Patrick concluded on his own. "This girl is really whacked out." Patricia had left once, driven away, but then "in no time the woman reappears in the house. My heart skipped a beat when I saw her standing in the doorway."

Patrick's intuitions were proved out early the following afternoon, when Patricia Bowman filed rape charges. Originally Bowman ostensibly asserted to detective Christine Rigolo that Senator Kennedy had watched Smith assault her; she then withdrew the claim, which would be discounted afterward by investigators as a "clerical error."

Within a day the story leaked. When Palm Beach police turned up at the mansion on Sunday most of the Kennedys were at Saint Edward's Roman Catholic Church for the Easter mass, after which they repaired to a nearby restaurant for Bloody Marys and lunch. At that point William Barry seems to have left the impression with the officers who came by La Guerida that William Smith and Edward Kennedy were already on their way to Washington, while Ted Kennedy himself, informed that the charge was "sexual battery," claimed that he had "no idea" who the plaintiff was, and supposedly did not make the connection to rape but rather assumed that the police were primarily concerned with a number of objets d'art which Patricia Bowman had carted off — a sizable urn, a note pad, and several small pictures. Patricia Bowman would insist that she had taken these objects to prove that she had visited the mansion; apologists for the Kennedys would bruit it about that the entire scenario was concocted to cover a theft.

Nevertheless, the family did not waste time before hiring a sharp local attorney and one-time drug prosecutor, Mark Schnapp, and instigating a counterattack. Private detectives stepped in to investigate the alleged victim's background. Patricia Bowman's stepfather, Michael G. O'Neil, turned out to be the former chairman of General Tire and Rubber, and he would make it plain right away that he was rich and infuriated enough to take the Kennedys on wholesale.

"Within three or four days" investigators on the Kennedy payroll had assembled "a picture of Patricia Bowman as somebody who used cocaine, ran around with cocaine dealers, had abortions, split up with the father of her child — that sort of thing," one reporter on the scene remembers. And they were not making it difficult for the press to share all that. By April 14 *The New York Times* had joined *The Boston Herald* and CBS News in naming the alleged rape victim, until then a taboo in establishment journalism. The feature in the *Times* dwelt on

Patricia's "wild streak," her seventeen driving tickets, her penchant for "fun with the ne'er-do-wells of cafe society." The Great Gray Lady was rocking with the tabloids.

It is a cliché of American political reportage that the public has no memory. But these days the media does, and it is murderous if selective. Rumor gets legitimized fast, and one evening's whisper turns into the morning's banner headline in *The New York Times,* frequently above the fold.

This is a process the astute *Boston Globe* feature writer John Aloysius Farrell has dubbed the "tabloidization of mainstream journalism." His editors in Boston got Farrell down to Florida the late March weekend in 1991 the rape charges surfaced with instructions to determine as fast as possible whether Kennedy himself was implicated. Farrell quickly satisfied himself that the senator would not be charged. "What I didn't anticipate," Farrell says now, "was that this would turn into a sort of huge chapter in the war between the sexes. . . . That it would be seen in Boston as a test of whether the *Globe* was finally going to cover the Kennedys hard, and that it would open this whole chapter of his private life which had only been vaguely hinted at if even mentioned in the *Globe* for thirty years."

"The whole thing turned into a media free-for-all," Farrell concludes. "This is the first instance that I can remember where the reporting in the supermarket tabloids made it to the newspaper tabloids and spilled through the wire services into the mainstream press so quickly. Kennedy's people were as shocked as I was."

Whichever angle you took, the tone and proportions of the imbroglio, this projection of privilege on a romp, brought down an unremitting press barrage. In Massachusetts in particular even the loyalists were irate. *The Boston Globe's* streetwise columnist Mike Barnicle, who over the decades so often had spoken up for Kennedy, had finally had enough: "Kennedy stated he was simply enjoying a 'traditional Easter weekend,' which makes you wonder what these people do to celebrate something like Father's Day. Wear towels and run after girls, the younger Kennedy men rounding up the handsome women and allowing the 59-year-old Teddy to cut one out of the crowd?"

"Surrounded by sycophants," Barnicle wound it up, "Edward Kennedy thinks his name and title are license to do whatever he wants, and apparently the only voice he hears in that dark, lonely time before danger calls is the drink saying: 'Go ahead. You can get away with anything.'"

Halfway through his indictment the astute Barnicle ventured a prognostication guaranteed to stop hearts across Capitol Hill. More of Kennedy's "core constituency disappears with each day's obituaries," Mike observed, and "next time out, if he indeed runs again, he will positively be beaten by any credible candidate with the money to wage a decent campaign."

It wouldn't be long before poll results vindicated Barnicle. The following July a *Boston Herald*-WCVB survey cited 62 percent of its respondents as of the opinion that Kennedy should not run for reelection in 1994. By 2-1 those replying to the pollster felt Kennedy misled Palm Beach authorities. Some 55 percent characterized Kennedy's job performance as fair to poor. Governor William Weld would beat Kennedy in a statewide election 59-34. Nearly half who answered would admit that they were less likely to vote for Kennedy in the wake of "his drinking and his actions in Palm Beach."

Around Boston and the District a number of the people Ted Kennedy had worked with and depended on his entire adult life were bracing themselves, unhappily, to walk away. "We'd like to see him recover enough to finish out his term with a little dignity and retire," one told me; another, with whom the senator had always conferred in any emergency, reported that this time he simply hadn't heard anything. Nor had he inquired. There really wasn't much to say.

10

The magazine press now fell to conducting a succession of autopsies in print of Kennedy's character. *Time* referred to the perception of Ted as a "Palm Beach boozer, lout and tabloid grotesque. . . ." *Newsweek* termed him "the living symbol of the family flaws." Hearsay and invective of an unexampled ferocity promptly found its way into the staidest publication; even the Chappaquiddick publicity, disastrous as it was, had been confined pretty largely to speculation about the accident.

A manuscript that Putnam intended to bring out was around New York in galleys. In it Rick Burke, Kennedy's office manager toward the end of the seventies and through his run at the Democratic nomination, presented his ex-boss as drug-soaked and uncontrollable much of the time, popping vials of amyl nitrate or snorting cocaine even with his children while grabbing after anything presentable. Kennedy's women Burke took the poetic liberty of presenting in "composite" form; in fact, after close chronological examination, contemporaries in Kennedy's offices attributed a number of Burke's details to the hallucinatory transports which landed him in a mental hospital after shooting out the windshield of his own car and demanding police protection against alleged assassins. After business reverses Burke needed money badly. Before publication Putnam scrubbed the book, which ultimately did appear as *The Senator* in 1992 under another publisher.

Charges from Burke's book started leaking, first into the tabloids and presently into the more accountable press. Such representations were hard to deflect in the face of the prevailing lava flow. Kennedy conceded to a reporter that he would "have to be a little more attentive to behavior," but insisted that he had "never felt that I have a [drinking] problem." A Senate ethics committee inquiry into Kennedy's actions as conduct which reflected badly on the Senate was lodged in June and dismissed after a week. In October Kennedy won the Claude Pepper Distinguished Service Award from his colleagues, and even nippy Minority Leader Robert Dole, while conceding his "disagreement with Ted on most of the public policy issues of the day," allowed as how he had "never doubted for a minute his commitment to help the elderly, the ill, and those Americans who have been on the outside looking in for far too long." This registered as something between an endorsement and a eulogy.

Kennedy's adult children stood by and tried to help, each in his own way. Teddy, who had just graduated from the Yale School of Forestry, now enrolled himself publicly in the drug and alcohol program at the Institute of Living at Hartford. "In my family and among my friends," he told a reporter, "I've seen what happens when people don't address the problem." *Which* people he did not need to specify. "I realized that nothing could be right when that part was wrong."

Kennedy bit his lip and attempted to face up. "I recognize my own shortcomings," he murmured to an audience at Harvard on October 25, "the faults in the conduct of my private life. I realize that I alone am responsible for them, and I am the one who must confront them." This hadn't come easily. Only Kennedy could comprehend the pressure building month by month, and what it took to lift it sometimes.

One price Kennedy's notoriety exacted became clear that fall during the Clarence Thomas hearings. Millions who had depended on Kennedy to nail down the social consequences, to pose the puncturing question, now watched him brooding through the rounds of inquiry with little to contribute. He looked painfully detached a lot of the time, and occasionally downright sheepish. Each time he did speak up he risked another round of digs by the pundits, of wholesale tabloid abuse. "Are we an old boys' club," he broke out once in defense of Anita Hill, "insensitive at best, and perhaps something worse? Will we strain to concoct any excuse? To impose any burden? To tolerate any insubstantial attack on a woman in order to rationalize a vote for this nomination?" But this resonated oddly, falling across a public which attributed to the senator negligence, at the very least, in the face of rape.

Kennedy weighed in another time to point out how "the vanishing views of Judge Thomas have become a major issue in these hearings," and added that Thomas's American Bar Association ratings were lower than those of Robert Bork, of Harold Carswell, of Clement Haynsworth. This reminded the cognoscenti that all three nominees had been denied Supreme Court seats through Kennedy's intervention.

Kennedy's staff director on Judiciary, Jeff Blattner, points out that Kennedy was never intended to play a central role in the Thomas hearings. Especially since 1988, when Judiciary's Chairman Joseph Biden was out for seven months with a brain aneurysm and Kennedy took over and directed the Committee according to *Biden's* priorities, the two have collaborated with an extraordinary mutual sensitivity. There was an understanding early that Democratic Senators Patrick Leahy of Vermont and Howell Heflin of Alabama would lead the questioning of Thomas, while Hatch of Utah and Arlen Specter of Pennsylvania would defend the nomination. Just then Kennedy's energies were absorbed with jockeying the Civil Rights Bill of 1991 through the Senate. The help of Jack Danforth of Missouri was critical; Danforth was Thomas's primary Senate sponsor.

Relegated to the back benches, Kennedy and his staff were admittedly a stroke or two behind in establishing how spotty Thomas's record was, how retrograde his opinions. Reliable allies in vital civil rights groups, especially the NAACP, tended to hang back rather than oppose early a fellow African-American, especially one the administration's "pinpoint strategy" was promoting hard as a battler from impoverished circumstances whose story of personal success must inspire and reassure.

Once Thomas started juking, repudiating the tangled and reactionary phrasemaking which represented his contribution to the literature, many of the senators had already come forward with support. "In hindsight," Blattner admits, "the lack of an effort on the part of opponents to make Judge Thomas's record and views clear early on proved to seriously undermine the ultimate effort to defeat his nomination." By then the supercharged sexual vaudeville over Thomas's alleged overtures to Anita Hill left everybody in sight shuffling toward the cloakroom.

Could Kennedy, unencumbered, have upended Clarence Thomas? "I'm convinced he could have," says one aide whose knack for extricating the Senate from a series of rotten Supreme Court choices goes back to dumping Harold Carswell. "Without the Palm Beach problem." Had they been free to crank up earlier, to enlist their constituencies. Thomas got in, narrowly, but over the following months Warren Rudman would repudiate his own vote over public television, and David Boren has expressed regrets, and Wyche Fowler was reportedly backpedaling. If Kennedy had indeed limited himself to a walk on the beach that fateful Easter weekend we might have been spared the prospect of Clarence Thomas's America.

In December the fever broke. Called to the witness stand at the rape trial of William Smith in West Palm Beach, Kennedy seemed forthcoming, calm, senatorial. The widely broadcast proceedings had permitted enough of the sensationalist detritus to settle to convince the broad public that Kennedy's involvement was unintended, peripheral. On December 11 a jury found William Smith innocent. An expertly mounted defense by his attorney, Roy Black, along with Smith's heartfelt and frequently embarrassing depiction of a series of sticky exchanges on the night beach, replete with partial ejaculations, half-healed bruises, incomplete tumescence, and too much or not enough sand in Patricia Bowman's panties ultimately convinced the jurors that what had happened was in all likelihood consensual. Smith's uncle gained back a measure of innocence by association.

If anything, Kennedy staffers agree, their boss seemed steadier than usual throughout the long ordeal. "Even during the rape trial, which must have been rock bottom," Dave Nexon says, "he still had the same zest, worked the same hours. . . ."

By 1991 the White House was blockading a lot of legislation. Under pressure from Republican moderates, Bush finally signed the Civil Rights Act of 1991 as well as the pioneering National Service proposal and the reauthorized Higher Education Act. But mossbacks and heavy campaign contributors around the country were now "beating up on Bush," remembers Kennedy's staff director on the Labor Committee Nick Littlefield, and John Sununu had just observed that "As far as I'm concerned, Congress can go home." There ensued a string of presidential vetoes which included the Family Leave bill, the Striker Replacement Bill, the Elementary and Secondary School Reform Act, (which Kennedy had shepherded through the Senate 92-6) and out to the reauthorization of the National Institute of Health.

One development which sustained Kennedy was a new romance. Sloe-eyed and chestnut-haired, Victoria Reggie was frank, sprightly, and comparatively young at thirty-eight. But she was different on impact from the maturing starlets and D.C. socialites whom Kennedy had been squiring in public for decades by then. She was patently authentic, an unabashed free spirit. Victoria's grandparents on both sides were immigrants from Beirut, Maronite Christians who settled into the small-town life of Crowley, Louisiana and pulled a heavy oar in the local Catholic Church while easing their children into business and politics. Victoria's mother, Doris, was an heiress to the Bunny Bread baking fortune. There was a warmth here, a sense of belonging, which could not help but appeal to Kennedy just then, living day to day once more as a national pariah.

Furthermore, Victoria's father, Judge Edmund Reggie, was an influential wheeler-dealing lawyer and close associate of the controversial governor Edwin Edwards. Reggie caught the eye of the younger Kennedys before they amounted to anything on the national level, at the 1956 convention which nominated Adlai Stevenson. Jack Kennedy was mounting an unsuccessful eleventh-hour effort to grab the vice-presidential slot from Estes Kefauver. Himself a delegate from Louisiana, the judge took immediately to Jack and Bobby, warmed by their "great Boston accents," Victoria relates, "as well as the fact that neither of them wore BrylCreem in their hair." When Russell Long disappeared for a few hours to find a drink, Reggie lined the delegation up behind John Kennedy.

For Victoria, like Ted, a lot of the fascination is in the all-too-human details. By 1960 Judge Reggie was managing a big section of the deep South for the Kennedys, and remained a powerful local retainer in 1968 and again in 1980. Kennedy found himself drawn to this spirited, tight-knit family, and particularly the judge, who was already fending off by 1982 what mounted to eleven federal indictments for fraud and mismanagement in a scramble to salvage his collapsing savings and loan holdings. Throughout a decade of battering in the courts Edmund Reggie remained beautifully turned out, solid behind Kennedy interests, and devoted but never obsequious. Reggie called Ted "The Commander," "because he's always ordering everybody else around all the time," and Kennedy just took it and chuckled and showed up regularly for more. The Reggies maintained a summer house on Nantucket, and Kennedy liked to sail over and visit them there.

For decades Kennedy barely noticed Victoria. She grew up happy in Crowley, one of the six Reggie children, a superstar in the local parochial school who developed so fast that her mother still thinks of her as getting "out of a chair in five or six different parts at a time." Graduating Phi Beta Kappa from Sophie Newcomb College, she was president of her sorority. At Tulane Law School she made the law review and graduated summa cum laude before deserting this paradise of Cajunburgers and catfish platters to put in a stint of clerking in the U.S. Seventh Circuit Court of Appeals in Chicago. She met her first husband — Grier Raclin, a low-keyed telecommunications attorney — with whom she had two children and moved to D.C. The marriage came apart and they were divorced in 1990.

Meanwhile, Victoria had become a partner in the Washington firm of Keck, Mahin and Cate. Her specialty was banking, particularly loan restructuring and workout. One colleague would characterize her as "charismatic and hard-driving," and popular with her clients. She developed a reputation for settlement negotiations during which no prisoners were taken, a memory for details it took her spontaneity and brio to keep from intimidating her contemporaries.

A colleague at Keck, Mahin who was also a familiar of Kennedy's, Peter Edelman, opens other possibilities: "She's smart, she's very funny, and you know how much he values being able to laugh. She's kind of outrageous in a wonderful way, very earthy. He's fortunate to have found her." In Victoria the fussy, demanding, daylight side of Kennedy's personality were met with a ripple of the Dionysian.

Throughout Kennedy's occasional visits to the Reggies, "We saw each other but then we didn't see each other," Victoria comments. Then, in June of 1991, Vickie gave a fortieth anniversary party for her parents in D.C. at her house on Woodley Park. Edmund invited The Commander, who showed up without a date. "I teased him about that," Victoria remembers, "and I guess the rest is history."

"Ted was a very nice, polite, dedicated suitor. Very very sweet and very considerate," Victoria says. "He always called me the day after a date to tell me he had a very nice time." Roses arrived by truckload. Victoria was working hard, she had natural hesitations, and it was important to her to spend as much time with her children as she could, so most evenings that summer she and Kennedy and Caroline, six, and Curran, nine, got together at Woodley Park. Victoria usually cooked — crawfish étouffé and grape leaves and tabouli are specialties — after which Kennedy was likely to slide down onto the floor with Caroline and help her with her coloring books.

Publicity from the Palm Beach affair was lighting up the media, but "we were in a very insulated situation," Victoria recalls. "It wasn't like the topic of dinner table conversation. We were just two people getting to know each other." Throughout the Smith trial Kennedy called her every day. "She was his solace away from the storm," one friend says. "It gave him confidence that she would be there during hard times."

When Kennedy finally decided to propose he braced himself and telephoned a few old friends, starting with John Tunney and John Culver. They were so unabashedly pleased — none of the usual needling, nothing but warmth and congratulations — that Kennedy followed up with calls to a few others and in the end reached dozens of people, including a string of one-time girlfriends and, by the end, Joan. Everybody wished him well. It was a job getting Kennedy off the telephone that afternoon.

Kennedy popped the question at the opera, Victoria remembers, and "I was very happy that he asked me." She knew that Kennedy was "a person who had been dating a great deal," as her father put it, she'd seen enough herself to conclude that his drinking wasn't going to pose a problem, and she was deeply in love. She understands Kennedy thoroughly. Any time he threatens to throw his weight around Vicki does not hesitate to tweak him about whether he really hadn't married her to get his poll results up. This is a marriage of passion between equals, the only arrangement possible for someone who insists cheerfully that "I have lived my life in terms of the empowerment of women."

Not that this inhibits Victoria from taking on touchier, more traditional assignments. With reelection in 1994 coming up, Vicki organized a reception in Boston for Ted for 1,200 influential New England women, importing five Democratic senators to demonstrate that Kennedy was holding his own in Washington. She put together a western-style barbecue when Teddy Jr. married Katherine Anne Gershman in October of 1993. To form some bond with Joan — who has been up and down — Victoria reportedly telephoned her and asked for advice about piano lessons for Caroline. Kennedy routinely includes Victoria in staff-run strategy sessions.

Merely talking about Ted lights up Victoria's impudent hazel eyes, thrusts forward her strong Levantine chin and nose. "Really, life's wonderful," Victoria Kennedy sums it up. "We laugh a lot, we definitely laugh a lot. I think I'm the luckiest woman on earth."

In Boston Cardinal Bernard Law continued to block Kennedy's appeal for an annulment of his marriage to Joan. But with or without the church, Kennedy went ahead and married Vicki in a small, private ceremony in July of 1992. By then Bill Clinton had long since locked up the Democratic nomination.

The relationship between Bill Clinton and Edward Kennedy had taken some months to come to a boil. Still wary about styling himself too far to the left, even in Massachusetts, Clinton skirted joint campaign appearances with the senator. The two men "don't really have a relationship," one Clinton aide told the press. Clinton was famously proud of the widely distributed photograph of himself as a Boy's Nation junior delegate shaking JFK's hand on a trip to Washington. Ted Kennedy had made it a point to telephone Clinton in Little Rock to congratulate — or console — him after each gubernatorial election, and Clinton would reciprocate by helping Kennedy's staff pull together background material implicating Robert Bork, a professor of Clinton's at Yale Law School.

But as a cofounder and chairman of the centrist Democratic Leadership Council, Clinton ducked too open an association with this Moloch of progressivism whom Republicans delighted in caricaturing as out to empty everybody's pocket into the public trough. Such perceptions of Kennedy were ludicrously out of date — had never meant very much — and

The end of Camelot is visible on the faces of the young Edward Kennedy and his sister Eunice in 1963 (above) as they leave the family aircraft, named after the dead ident's young daughter, Caroline. Looking on are Ted's wife Joan and the original oline. By 1967 Ted Kennedy (below) found himself again laboring in a brother's ow — this time Bobby's, the new junior senator from New York.

In May 1980, challenging Jimmy Carter in the presidential primaries, Kennedy (above) called in vain on the president to confront him in debate. The lingering effects of Chappaquiddick, and the mistakes of Kennedy and his campaign managers, ultimately doomed his effort, but in return for supporting Carter at the Democratic convention (below, with aides Carey Parker in the rear and Robert Shrum behind microphone), Kennedy was given unprecedented control over the party platform.

ed's brother-in-law Steve Smith (far right above with wife Jean and President Corazon Aquino of the Phillipines at a Kennedy Library event in 1986) managed Kennedy family money and played a major role in every Kennedy campaign. One d's principal aides was Carey Parker (below, 1987), a legislative assistant who dou-as overall idea man and speech editor.

On Easter weekend the year after Steve Smith's death in 1990, his son William tering West Palm Beach County Courthouse above in November 1991) went drinking with Uncle Ted and Cousin Patrick. A rape charge by the young wo Willy brought back to the Kennedy family compound in Palm Beach domin headlines for months. Ted (on his way to court with sister Pat Lawford be November 1991) found his personal life under intense public scrutiny.

omestic legislation was always Ted Kennedy's first concern but he maintained contact with the world's leaders — those waiting in the wings as well as those in er. He introduced Nelson and Winnie Mandela to his delighted son, Patrick ove), and with Jackie Onassis (below, in 1992) welcomed Eduard Shevardnadze, bachev's Foreign Minister during the last days of the Soviet Union.

Kennedy depends heavily on staffers like Melody Miller, his deputy press [secretary] (above, accompanying the senator in 1992 to the John F. Kennedy Librar[y in] Boston for the annual Profiles in Courage Award presentation). Years of bad publ[icity] made Kennedy unexpectedly vulnerable in the 1994 senatorial race, when he was c[hal]lenged by businessman Mitt Romney (below) who flagged during the final weeks.

espite wariness on both sides, Ted Kennedy and Bill Clinton (above with JFK's children John and Caroline and Bobby's son Joseph in 1993) maintained a work- relationship during President Clinton's first term. Another ascendant Democrat) has remained close to Kennedy is Tom Daschle, currently the Senate's Minority der (with Ted in 1996 on the porch of JFK's birthplace).

As a champion of traditional Democratic Party values, Ted Kennedy fought har
1995 (above) to limit proposals for budget cuts in entitlements which woul
the middle class and working poor. Friends agree that the senator's personal life
been unusually calm since his marriage in 1993 to Victoria Reggie (below), daught
a longtime political ally of the Kennedys.

behind the scenes Kennedy helped where he could to promote Clinton's candidacy. Kennedy strategists, from Paul Tully and Bill Carrick to Rick Stearns and Ron Brown, signed on with Clinton, along with office specialists like Kennedy's foreign policy aide Nancy Soderberg. But relations remained arms-length.

What brought the two politicians together in the end was the exploding health issue. The off-year Senate triumph in 1991 in Pennsylvania of longtime Kennedy spear carrier Harris Wofford flagged health abuses across America. What Kennedy managed, over decades of concern, was largely to pinpoint the emerging inequities in the medical delivery system and suggest new solutions. Kennedy initiatives dating back to the end of the sixties had underscored the maldistribution of health care nationwide, the inappropriateness that we, the richest Western nation, should remain the only major industrialized society without universal health coverage. Disagreements with the Carter administration over both the urgency and the timing of health reform had more than anything else inveigled Kennedy into running in 1980.

Along with his West Virginia colleague Jay Rockefeller and Henry Waxman in the House, Kennedy kept the drumbeat alive throughout the Reagan years — his bills would range from attacks on the administration for starving out research to demands for limits on overbilling by hospitals and doctors to defenses of "family planning options" to bipartisan resolutions to bring the "37 million uncovered Americans into the health care system" by way of state and employer mandates.

This last proposal surfaced in 1986. Kennedy had long since given up on looking to the federal government — the "single payer" — and acknowledged that the best chances of passage lay in propitiating the insurance interests. Between his opposition to the disclosure provisions of the administration's AIDS package as an "invitation to drive the epidemic underground and encourage its spread" and year after year of scattered hearings to point up such suppressed outrages as the prevalence of leukemia at nuclear reactor sites, Kennedy kept the spotlight moving. He pressed for "Lifecare," nursing facilities for the deteriorating elderly. He fought for the right of health care workers to bring up abortion during family planning sessions.

More than anything else, Kennedy recognized that irresponsible policymaking in the insurance industry was compounding the panic. In April of 1992 Kennedy spelled it out before the Health Insurance Association of America: "Your private sector role has unquestionably made the crisis worse," he leveled at them. "The message sent out by too many of your member companies is unmistakably clear: don't insure anyone unless you think they won't get sick. And if you make a mistake, do your best to walk away from it. Do all you can to stop Congress from acting. . . ."

What Kennedy laid before Hillary Clinton and her task force in 1993 was literally decades of spadework, numberless hearings and staff studies and libraries full of expert testimony already subjected to analysis and ready to translate into legislation. "The senator decided early on to cooperate as closely with the president as he could," emphasized Dave Nexon, Kennedy's health staff director. "He likes Clinton, they're on the same wavelength. The administration invited our Hill staff to come in and cooperate, and after a while we had ten people involved, everybody, including the fellows. I personally spent 90 percent of my time down there. Hillary is phenomenal. . . ."

It wasn't really a stretch for either Kennedy or Clinton, who quickly embroidered on their older-brother/kid brother material. "Kennedy has been reinventing government, reexamining traditional liberal positions for a long time," one senior in both camps suggests. "There isn't any sense of, 'Gee, *I* should have been there.' Look at all those people having their prima donna ways — Sam Nunn, David Boren, Dave McCurdy. You know, there are aspects of the Clinton proposals Kennedy is not so pleased with, especially the public health side of the legislation — what happens to low income people, chronically ill children, mental health. You'll see him press his points in some way — from the inside. He understands that the president and Hillary see the whole playing field, the pressures and counterpressures. . . ."

Grateful, Bill Clinton has shown a flattering receptivity to the Kennedys during White House functions. Jean Smith — cooling down after a reportedly quite bitter go-around with her kid brother coming out of the Palm Beach crunch — went on to Ireland as U.S. ambassador. Kowtows continue both ways.

There have been awkward moments as well during the appointments process. Kennedy was obviously nonplussed at the way the White House bumped ailing Circuit Court Justice Stephen Breyer, once a Kennedy aide and the prime mover behind airline and truck deregulation, from a Supreme Court nomination in June of 1993 after hauling him out of a hospital bed while Kennedy was trading chits with senators Dole and Hatch to lock Breyer in. Kennedy claimed to sympathize with these "tough, close decisions," by the president, but added, dejectedly, "He's a friend. Steve's a friend, so I can understand his disappointment."

Clinton, rarely dropping a beat, made it a point to address a Kennedy fund-raiser in Massachusetts later in the month. "Every effort to bring the American people together across that which divides us," the president asserted, "every effort has the imprint of Ted Kennedy." Clinton ticked off Kennedy's accomplishments merely in the previous twelve months. In his turn, Kennedy proclaimed that "We have waited for this president for twelve long years. We in Massachusetts are going to stump for the president's economic program, for his health program, and we are going to get him reelected."

Kennedy meant that. He functioned as the floor manager of Clinton's National Service plan, which cleared the Senate 54-40. He worked a complicated double-shuffle on Arlen Specter and his law-and-order Republicans that drove through the prohibition against blockading abortion clinic entrances without jeopardizing striker's rights. He sponsored a bill to let the federal government — not banks — finance student loans, saving undergraduates many millions. Wherever the battle was thickest, Clinton's first year, Kennedy was most likely to show up early. When Clinton returned to Boston to help open the Stephen E. Smith Center at the Kennedy Library, Joe Kennedy II came out publicly for NAFTA and grabbed his uncle's shoulder: "Are you listening to this?" Ted, fearful of his labor support, broke into a grin and turned his tie around like a hangman's noose. But in the end he took a breath and voted with Clinton on NAFTA.

As month after month throughout 1993 the Clinton administration's health bill foundered, Kennedy pushed his own collateral proposals through the Health Committee in an effort to salvage as much as possible and impart to the issue recovered momentum. Simultaneously, Kennedy jacked up federal support — from $34 to $65 billion — for medical education and teaching hospitals, a major industry in Massachusetts. Here was a program Hillary had initially proposed to cut; Bill Clinton personally reversed the administration's position, concedes one insider, "to avoid having surgery performed on his bill in Teddy's committee." One hand still washes the other, even among friends.

Successes were racking up; nevertheless — this must be said — there was a suspicion among hard-core liberals that Kennedy was trimming his principles more week by week to propitiate Clinton's Democratic Leadership corner-cutters. That in his desperation to escape the enduring Palm-Beach fallout he would consent to anything to get his name on bills. Although in the end, testifying at the Smith trial in December of 1991, Kennedy came through as measured, statesmanlike, tangential to the scandal, the public would remain divided over the verdict of innocence. The shadow was ominously slow to pass. "Republicans at the time told me that there was this sort of feeling that Kennedy could be had," notes one close observer. Concessions to Strom Thurmond on the Crime Bill left civil libertarians upset.

Purists singled out Kennedy's receptivity to hallowed Republican initiatives like the line-item veto along with his frankness in terming the budget process "a shambles." In an age of one-issue candidates he continued to insist that "We are citizens first and constituencies second."

Such positions were noble enough, but now they tended to soften Kennedy's edges. There was a suspicion building that Ted was losing his ideological fire. Others across the spectrum — Sam Nunn, Daniel Moynihan, Howard Metzenbaum — whatever the range of their beliefs, still seemed to stand for something throughout the Party. Like his NAFTA waffling, Kennedy's flexibility on the health issue — the same issue that provoked him into challenging Jimmy Carter for bringing forward a set of proposals a lot more substantive than anything Bill Clinton is likely to sign — raised hackles in labor halls.

By then it hadn't gone unnoticed that, of the $9.2 million Kennedy's discontinued Fund for a Democratic Majority had raised over the previous decade, less than a million was ever paid out directly to underwrite other Democrats.

Most onlookers would concede that Ted had all but single-handedly staved much of the Reagan Revolution off. But that was then. Was there anything left?

A fund-raiser in June of 1993 produced $500,000 in re-election money for Kennedy, cash he would need. Perceived as vulnerable, there was a compounding list of potential Republican challengers to Kennedy, led off by Governor William Weld and ex-Secretary of Transportation Andrew Card and — a rising threat — George Romney's son Mitt. A *Boston Globe* poll that spring pegged the Massachusetts voters at 41 percent favorable to Kennedy, 40 percent unfavorable. Kennedy let it be known, according to the *Globe,* that he "hoped people sense what his marriage last July has meant to him." Meanwhile, the federal government was winding up a decade of litigation against Kennedy's new father-in-law. In September Judge Edmund Reggie would plead nolo contendere to a misapplication of funds charge and subject himself to 120 days of home detention, three years of probation, and a $30,000 fine.

Public wrath was lifting: redemption was in the wind. Kennedy's mastery of pork-barreling had generated a range of federal subsidies to the financially hard-pressed Commonwealth, from billions to construct the Central Artery tunnel and clean up Boston Harbor to $29 million for the Center for Photonomics Research at Boston University which Kennedy tucked into a 1991 defense appropriations bill along with timely intervention to salvage a huge Martin Marietta plant.

The afternoon the Clintons visited Jackie Onassis on Martha's Vineyard in 1993, Kennedy waited until he had the president out on the water before pitching not only his own ideas about health but also the urgency of awarding a new Department of Defense accounting facility to troubled nearby Southbridge.

With reelection coming up, all politics reverts. Between legislative sessions and into the winter of 1994, Kennedy had been pounding through Massachusetts. Campaigning remains a grind — "The fun goes out of it, you end up in sweaty hotel rooms seeing nothing but one television crew after another," Kennedy warned his nephew Joe in 1986 — but Ted can still find ways to liven up the afternoons. Rolling up to a mob of construction workers while canvassing the Commonwealth late in 1993, Kennedy's office manager Paul Donovan divulges, the senator cranked a window down and shouted across the havoc: "Listen, you fellows, go take the rest of the day off. Tell 'em the senator said it was OK."

That Kennedy was emerging from the pall became clear from the press reception of Joe McGinniss's long-dreaded biography of the senator, *The Last Brother*. The book was exceedingly tough on Kennedy, and spiked with insupportable supposition. But at its richest moments McGinniss's study did indeed project a fascinating rendition of the Kennedys as a "Dysfunctional Poster Family," in Ellen Goodman's words, alternately driven and self-indulgent, and in the end recklessly self-destructive.

What made the book most notable was the extent to which the reviewing organs savaged it. It was as if the opinion-makers who two years earlier simply could not dig up enough with which to foul Kennedy's reputation now colluded to sanctify the remains. The roast was over.

It was as if the nation as well as the Congress finally understood that, blowoffs and all, Kennedy was ultimately irreplaceable. Wounds healed. Kennedy made a point of stepping back when his press nemesis Rupert Murdoch bought the bankrupt *New York Post,* and before long even Murdoch's *Boston Herald* had to admit that Kennedy was in fact Massachusetts' outstanding advocate in Congress. By October of 1993 Kennedy's "admiration level" had crept up to 58 percent. The crisis seemed over.

12

In politics too often admiration doesn't guarantee electability. By mid-spring of 1994, with reelection in Massachusetts coming up, the needles of prognosis were jumping in their seismographs. Much more than money was already involved. "Tell me," one gruff old loyalist from JFK's aging entourage demanded of me without warning over dinner. "Would you say that in Teddy's case there are enough brain cells left, for Christ's sake, to get him through a real campaign? He'd have to debate Mitt Romney.

"There are a lot of people in Massachusetts — and these are people who really don't have anything against Teddy, they think he's done the job. But at the same time they haven't forgotten Palm Beach, and *I* think a helluva lot of them feel that it's gotten to be — you know — gold watch time."

A few weeks earlier, a *Boston Globe* poll had concluded that while 60 percent of the electorate still regarded Kennedy favorably, only 38 percent felt that he merited another term, while 62 percent felt that it was time for somebody else. A mainstay for Kennedy Democrats for decades, new ownership and a shakeup on the *Globe's* editorial page left even its support in question.

The crust was thin suddenly; beneath everything oblivion boiled.

At that stage George Romney's telegenic son Mitt was rounding into favor as the Republican nominee. Kennedy himself still tended to dismiss the increasingly serious challenge, resorting to his familiar dictum that he intended to campaign *for* his established principles, not *against* any particular individual. This meant he still regarded himself as comfortably ahead.

Nevertheless, he had been packing his weekends with extra days of campaigning around the Commonwealth. One Monday toward the end of June I arranged to join Kennedy's party. It had been sultry all weekend on the Cape, miasmal, but during the previous few hours the heat wave across New England had taken a turn. Although the sun was out a breeze was up, and windows in the van were open. "My God, what weather!" Kennedy exclaimed while the van pulled out, twisting against his safety belt on the passenger side to confront the middle seats. He tipped his Orange Slice up, straight out of the can. "Those guys back there, they know what they're doin'," Kennedy announced. "They do it well, there's really a sense of pride."

We were just pulling away from an hour at the GE jet-engine plant at Lynn, a classic campaign stopover, divided between buttering up the executives and joshing and hand-shaking the senator's jovial way along the echoing plant floor. For all the computer-driven lathes from Cincinnati Milacron and display tables decked out with mirror-finish turbine discs, there persisted a reliable nineteenth-century stolidity to the place. Heavy machinery grinding away made normal conversation impossible; the smell of cutting oil off mountains of scrolled-steel shavings flattened out the stale trapped air.

"In all the time I've been on the Armed Services Committee," Kennedy had been careful to reassure the management during his short address, "no matter where the frames come from, the engines are GE — Lynn." Behind him, mounted like a trophy, a prototype jet engine gleamed, dominant throughout the industry.

What sticks with Kennedy, reminiscing in the van, is what lives tending those huge gray machines have amounted to, what people's prospects are. "Did you hear that union rep telling me that they can produce a casting in there right now in one day that used to take them sixteen days?" Kennedy wonders, at large. "It's mind-boggling. They have an incentive system — that's what this guy was tellin' us — they get the bonuses. The corporate guys just sort of stand there writing this stuff down. . . ."

Industrial America was coming around. "I remember in '68," Edward Kennedy laughs, "they had these *tanning factories* up here on the North Shore. The parts would come in from Australia. Big wood barrels, filled with hides and acid. So many things you can't remember, but this I can remember as if it were yesterday.

"I'd gone through on two different occasions. They gave you these big rubber overshoes to put on, because otherwise the acid would eat the threads in your shoes. So, the second time I didn't put the overshoes on, and the next morning the soles of my shoes peeled right off. Like Band-Aids. Because the acid sits *this thick* on the floor of the place, and here these people are right in it all day, and they are touchin' it, and bending over and scratchin' themselves. . . . And I noticed their teeth — all cavities, and comin' out of their mouths at every angle. It wasn't long after that that I got a ten million dollar fluoridation bill through — after all, you know, they fluoridated in Brookline and Newton, and they haven't had a cavity there since. I thought — if that was happening *down*town—"

Kennedy guffaws. There *is* a difference to be made. Churning up the hustings, seeding in his '94 Senate reelection, Kennedy picks up energy steadily bumping around the State. His schedule is packed with opportunities to merchandise what seniority can do for biotech engineers and computer hardware entrepreneurs, to dispense block grant money and ARPA — Advanced Research Products Agency — checks to CEOs across the North Shore.

Between appearances he gets to relax. "Hey, big guy," he rounds on his amused driver after a wrong turn. "This is unbelievable. If you were lookin' at the map instead of tryin' to tickle me, we wouldn't be on this side street. And where's the little orange juice can? Have you drunk that already?"

Refreshment is where you grab the opportunity. A few minutes later, wandering through the laboratories of the Abiomed Company in Danvers, Kennedy plucks up a plastic and titanium artificial heart the size of a cantaloupe and presses it against the narrow chest of a skinny little local photographer for fit. "Don't get sick," he advises the astonished cameraman. "Me, it's all right."

Kennedy's heft these days is again a concern to staffers in an election year, but he seems untroubled. There is old pol's ambiance about Kennedy this time around, a degree of comfort that, closing in on sixty-three, he has at last evolved into what he needs to be. The day grows warmer and warmer, but

Kennedy rocks in and out of the factory gates and conference rooms and cafeterias of post-industrial Massachusetts, his winter-weight double-breasted dark gray suit badly rumpled, shooting the big gold links in his French cuffs, increasingly red-faced and perspired. His heavy silver hair is cut quite wavy and long. Mature, foreshortened by the decades, he's come to resemble the Toby Mug version of himself.

Still — settled in, listening to the presentations from executives who want something from their government, Kennedy betrays underlying restlessness. He drums his fingers, draws scimitars on his note pad and inks each blade in slowly, pulls off his big chrome-rimmed bifocals and opens and closes the bows a few times and slides them into his pocket and glances around balefully from under those grizzled scrollwork brows and pulls the glasses out and smudges them up and puts them on and takes them off again. When formalities are over, and Kennedy has made his pitch for health care and the crime bill in front of the mandatory assemblage of secretaries and technicians, there remains just one more item: "By the way," he reminds his onlookers, "there is an election this fall. And Vicki here would like to see her husband reelected."

Something unexpected was starting to be felt. Ted Kennedy could lose.

Back in the van, Kennedy sidesteps direct questions about the presumptive challenger, W. Mitt Romney, a wealthy venture capitalist and president of the Boston stake, its fourteen Mormon Churches. All through the Commonwealth politics is traditionally retail, tribal, and today is one more investment by Kennedy in the effort to persuade local chiefs that he can indeed do more for Massachusetts — and for them — after which the word was expected to go forth among the Indians. Romney, on the other hand, seemed determined to buy up Kennedy's Senate seat wholesale, through recurrent television blanketings, in expectation of bypassing the ancient constituencies and pulling in voters electronically.

And this was working. After having trailed other candidates prior to the May 19 preferential primary, Romney bombarded the airwaves with spots which presented him as a breathtakingly clean-cut forty-seven-year-old father of five "healthy" sons, well suited to demolish the exhausted incumbent. Republican delegates promptly conferred on him 68 percent of their votes. There remained the formal Republican primary in September, and aspirant businessman John Lakian intended to square off against Romney one more time. Mitt Romney looked practically unstoppable.

Whereas in the past Ted's "strategy has always been to raise plenty of money early," observed Milton Gwirtzman, a tuner of political pianos for the Kennedys since Jack, "and get the momentum up enough to scare anybody of substance out," the three or four million dollars the Kennedy campaign had raised so far did not look at all intimidating against the $8 million the Romneys had pledged. As the primary dealmaker for Bain Capital, the venture capital arm of Bain and Company, Romney was widely reported to pull in more than $6 million in a successful year, over ten times Ted's income. Romney's approach was forthright: "If people believe the answer to America's problems is more government, then they should vote for Ted Kennedy. He's the expert on government."

Out on the road again and headed toward Peabody, I managed to nudge Kennedy into touching on — reluctantly, and in that notorious semicoherent delivery he resorts to when he is censoring himself — his apprehensions about the Romney candidacy: "You know, in a state that's hard-pressed economically, the situation has powerful forces that are, uh, out there, that are looking for simplistic kinds of responses. . . ." He named no names. Nevertheless, "I'm going to welcome the opportunity for people to debate me on these issues if they are serious about them."

I 3

The day will come when aficionados of political science will climb all over this most expensive and embattled of Kennedy's reelection campaigns with the kind of game-plan cross-analysis the smart pros hold back until they are dealing with a classic. This fight had everything — religious haymakers above and below the belt, money panics, the drama of youth versus age, lifestyle clash. That summer and into the fall the recession-ridden Commonwealth heaved.

The balance kept shifting. Through June and into July Romney repeatedly reminded onlookers of the bathing beauty who had the contest won until she opened her mouth. In mid-June, attempting to pin up his own positions as contrasted with Kennedy's, Romney recommended a thirteen-point program he labeled "learn-fare," kept rigorous by requiring drug testing for welfare recipients, mandatory employment for "able-bodied adults without dependents," and denial of all benefits to illegal aliens. It had escaped Romney that as matters stood only adults with dependents *were* welfare-eligible and that in Massachusetts nobody *could* collect welfare unless registered with the Immigration and Naturalization Service.

For someone who regularly claimed to run *for* the office, not against the challenger, Kennedy's response was anything but impersonal: "One of my two potential opponents, who made $11.6 million in the last two years, issued his first comprehensive position paper, attacking poor children and poor women — and he got it wrong."

Off on the wrong foot, Romney waded in deeper. In early July Romney characterized Kennedy as opposed to the line-item veto, against the Gramm-Rudman federal budget restrictions, in favor of single-payer health coverage, and soft on crime. In virtually every particular Mitt Romney had Kennedy's voting record backward.

Romney was soon compounding his research problem by attempting to straddle what positions he did take. *The Boston Globe's* in-house reactionary, Jeff Jacoby, came away from a *Globe* working lunch with Mitt and observed that he "looked good, spoke well, and came down firmly on both sides of almost every issue." Kennedy, weeks earlier, had accepted his party's nomination at the Worcester Centrum by reiterating, "plainly and unequivocally, that I welcome the opposition of the far right, the National Rifle Association, the anti-choice lobby, those who resist civil rights and equal rights." Republican columnist John Ellis pronounced the Romney campaign in "full flounder," and wondered whether "Romney isn't playing at a level well above his game." As the month ended Kennedy registered a 16-20 point lead in the polls.

Out ahead, Kennedy relaxed. His nephew, Robert Kennedy's son Michael, was responding well as campaign manager to jabs from the Republican aspirants; with luck this campaign might yet hold expenditures down to $2½-3 million, roughly what they budgeted. They cut back sharply on television.

Yet Kennedy's own advisors could see that there was a kind of quicksand under voters' perception of the boss: once he stopped moving, he was likely to sink. Kennedy's personal approval rating clearly undermined his job approval rating. This took the form of a widespread fixation on Kennedy's appearance, as if the reporters in particular could not forgive him for showing his age. Just after the convention one commentator decided that "The Old Lion was a little short in the Raw Meat Department," while another pronounced it "a flat, windy, partly recycled effort, delivered with an occasional grandfatherly quaver."

Romney's sound bytes played on this. One spot that cycled through the later months contrasted the vibrant Mitt, in rich color, with footage of Kennedy in grainy black and white, disheveled, paunchy and unsure, gingerly attempting to ease his back onto a park bench. This reinforced that summer's cliché identifying Kennedy as a street vagrant in a thousand-dollar suit. Kennedy's own ads regularly showed him hugging the winsome Victoria, as if to invigorate his image with her youth and vitality. "It's not that subtle," commented the *Globe's* AD-WATCH journalist Renee Loth. "All that's missing from this picture is Lassie."

By then, finally, Mitt Romney had identified his issue. He insisted that Kennedy was soft on crime, and had in fact "porked up" and watered down the $33 billion crime bill while leaving out new police and new prisons. Kennedy's longstanding opposition to the death penalty was hurting him. A belated round of ads featured Kennedy insisting that "The greatest threat we face is no longer overseas, but here on our streets," while a reassuring voice-over intoned: "He wrote the law that

abolished parole for federal crimes and denies bail for dangerous defendants."

Romney came back hard. "He's got to be kidding," one ad
responded. "For thirty-two years, Ted Kennedy has repeatedly
opposed tough crime measures, like the death penalty. . . ."
Romney's popularity readings surged.

Back in the District it was a muggy summer. The long-
awaited crime bill lost its first time around, caught up
in charges that provisions like funding midnight basketball
amounted to welfare in disguise. Romney's charges gained
more credibility. Before August was over the omnibus health
reform bill that Hillary and her minions had labored over since
arriving in the White House never made it to a floor vote in
the Senate, its 1,368-page welter of health-care alliances and
national health controls easy picking for the insurance industry's hatchet-wielding TV spokespeople Harry and Louise.

The collapse of health reform amounted to a setback for
Kennedy on a scale with the 1980 primary. Once Clinton took
office the language was waiting in draft at Labor and Human
Resources to effectuate at least the rudiments of universal
coverage, the Kennedy-Mitchell-Rockefeller proposal. Polls
showed how eager the public was to cover the 37 million
un-insured, and Kennedy and his co-sponsors had worked
the cloakroom to win over many Republicans, queasy at the
prospect of breasting an incoming tide of national expectations.
The way was open, had the inexperienced president only
moved in expeditiously behind Kennedy's preliminary deal-
making the way he had in the cases of AmeriCorps legislation
and student loans and job retraining.

"It would have passed by eighty-five votes in the Senate
those early months," one close observer maintains. Even after a
year and a half of special-interest sandpaper on the Clinton

plan's salient proposals, Kennedy's nose-counters were sure they could have eked out fifty-one supporters. But health by then was definitely a Hillary issue, swelling egos were involved. Worn out by more than a year spent providing close support operations to Hillary's overblown task force, top Kennedy staffers muttered openly about White House ineptitude. "The fact is, Ira Magaziner and to a certain extent Hillary Clinton were politically tone-deaf," one player maintains.

In June Kennedy had shepherded the repeatedly delayed Clinton plan through his own committee 11-6, still agitating to expand coverage for the poor as well as the disabled and women while developing a control mechanism to retard the growth of premiums. Dubbed "Clinton Heavy," Kennedy's version was subjected to public attack from Daniel Moynihan and the Finance Committee, alarmed at the prospective costs. Moynihan promulgated his Lite version. With right-wing PACs and small-business lobbyists stuffing mailboxes and bombarding the media, conservative Democrats gradually started to defect. Panicking, Clinton made it plain that virtually every aspect of his bill was "negotiable"; a stampede began, and by mid-August this opportunity of a generation had turned into a legislative rout.

Rolling around the Massachusetts hustings, Kennedy made it plain how deeply he continued to be invested in the issue. "Many companies now have wellness programs," I watched him explaining that summer of 1994 to a gaggle of flat-panel lithography technicians. "The fact of the matter is that their people live longer and they cost the health system more. That doesn't mean that we ought to hand out cigarettes." To one listener's observation that things weren't looking so good by then in Congress, Kennedy observed bravely that the country was "further down the road than you'd think from the newspapers. Whenever universal coverage actually gets to the floor, there develops this irresistible support for the bill. . . . When I get back down there we're going to propose that everybody in Massachusetts have the same program that I have. Let all my fellow members vote, just ask them: why don't you reject yours? People are paying attention. After all, in 1964 there were more votes for Medicare in the fall than in the previous spring. . . ."

All this was whistling in the dark, of course. Universal coverage was dead. Political virtuoso that he is, Bill Clinton was careful to turn up in Massachusetts for a well-publicized signing of the Kennedy-crafted $60 billion Elementary and Secondary Education Act. The president fluffed off his own State Department to let the Sinn Fein's spokesman Gerry Adams into the United States on a visa, arranged by Nancy Soderberg in good part as a personal sop to Ambassador to Ireland Jean Kennedy Smith. But nothing brought health back.

Sensing a momentum shift, the Romney campaign now went after Kennedy on grounds that he had not brought enough federal money to Massachusetts, that $1 went out for every $.97 federal programs provided. In his desultory way, Massachusetts Republican Governor William Weld bobbed up and risked an opinion: "I'm sure there have been a lot of things he [Kennedy] has done over the years," Weld remarked. "I'm not familiar with them." Just then Kennedy's constituent liaison staffers were very busy prodding along the federally financed $5 billion artery tunnel as well as the $100 million Boston Harbor cleanup project, not to mention the $150,000 they freed up so Weld could fund his own Washington office. But Weld's comment catered to the notion that Kennedy was played out even in Washington, ineffective.

Kennedy's eulogy in May of 1994 at Jackie Onassis's funeral had energized with what the Boston politicos call a "death bump" his expiring reputation. Even then his oration betrayed what was on his mind. "Teddy, you do it," he quoted his sister-in-law as urging him to greet the Clintons when they dropped by Jackie's Vineyard estate in 1993 for lunch. "Maurice [Templesman] isn't running for reelection."

A year later, Kennedy had pointedly abstained from joining the Clintons during their vacation on the Cape. He was not along the week the president visited Ireland. Exchanges with the White House remained amiable — after the disastrous history of skirmishes with Lyndon Johnson and Jimmy Carter, decent relations with a Democratic president looked like a prerequisite for survival — but distance opened up.

It did not help that 1994 marked the twenty-fifth anniversary of the Chappaquiddick incident. "This has been a tragedy which I've expressed responsibility for and which I live with every day of my life," Kennedy responded in mid-July to one more press-conference sortie. Older voters recalled Chappaquiddick; their descendants, gibed Republican political consultant Todd Domke, regarded Kennedy as "just an old career pol, a cultural joke. . . . To them, he's the oldest living juvenile delinquent in the country." Joan picked that moment to retain Monroe Inker, perhaps the Commonwealth's scrappiest divorce lawyer, to reopen her 1982 divorce settlement with Ted. Kennedy's poll results slid steadily; a reputable poll taken on September 8–9 gave Romney 43 percent to Kennedy's 42 percent.

———

This triggered a red alert. With two months left, Kennedy unhappily doubled his campaign budget and hired on several key Dukakis political managers, Charles Baker, John Sasso, and Jack Corrigan. Rick Gureghian, the campaign's fire-eating press aide, told reporters that upcoming Kennedy ads will "thoroughly explore" Romney's "hidden record" as a businessman. A day later Representative Joe Kennedy had jumped in and attacked the Mormon Church for excluding blacks and women from leadership positions while labeling Bain Capital as "a white boy's club." Evidently Massachusetts' lion of liberalism craved raw meat after all.

Eons before, in May, Kennedy waved aside Romney's Mormonism as "not an issue, and it shouldn't be. President Kennedy and the American people settled that issue in the 1960 campaign." But scruples have a way of bending under the pressure of long, close campaigns, and the fact remained that the high-flown Latter-Day Saints could clearly be made to seem at once prim and exotic somehow, uneasy-making to lunchbucket voters. The Kennedy campaign had already retained The Investigative Group, Inc., a detective agency headed by former Watergate deputy counsel Terry Lenzner. Meanwhile, Kennedy brought back the unflappable Jimmy Flug to coordinate opposition research.

Information had been surfacing for months — and leaking into features on Romney in the *Globe* — which tied Bain Capital to questionable backers. Close relatives of Orlando de Sola, a Salvadoran expatriate who had sponsored Major Roberto Aubuisson and his murderous Arena Party, provided seed money to Bain. Through arms-length exchanges, cash came from junk bonds Michael Milken underwrote several months after the SEC had filed suit against him. Other sources of investment ranged from Yale University to Robert Maxwell. All this wasn't easy to translate into attack spots, but certainly it encouraged some hope that claims of Romney's immaculate political conception were overstated.

While attempting to keep his distance from the born-again Christian Right, Romney had built his publicity image around home and family. He continued to bridle at questions that went to his Mormon affiliation, but the fact remained that, as a bishop in Cambridge and Belmont and subsequently the president of the Boston stake, Mitt obviously bore responsibility for decisions by his church. This subject he refused to discuss, rebuking reporters for bringing up matters like the unwillingness of the elders in Salt Lake City to admit women into the upper administrative levels or the elite priesthood.

Kennedy, in early September, put forth his opinion that the time had come to ordain women as Catholic priests. A local Catholic spokesman roared back within days: "It would have been surprising if Senator Kennedy had issued a statement to the contrary. It is entirely consistent with his lack of fidelity to Catholicism. . . ." Was Ted in the running for pope these days? Still, who lived in which church's pocket was out there for the voters.

By then a summer of coverage was beginning to probe the cracks in Romney's Oh-golly delivery and do-gooder manner. Appalled at the number of gays in his own congregation, Romney had as recently as the fall of 1993 reportedly denounced homosexuality as "perverse and reprehensible," and sex outside marriage as immoral. Now, Mitt would insist that he really meant pedophilia and sadomasochism. But doubts lingered. One member of his ward, Judy Dushku, a local government professor, observed: "I'm afraid Mitt's grown up with this sense of entitlement not to be criticized, and to interpret criticism as never constructive, and as always coming from the enemy. I think this is very dangerous for a political leader."

Near the end of August a single mother in Romney's stake gave an interview to the press in which she maintained that, a decade before, Romney had dropped by in the midst of her pregnancy to threaten her with excommunication if she didn't give up the baby for adoption through a church agency. Romney would dispute her interpretation of the incident. She kept the baby, and nobody in fact had excommunicated her, yet Romney himself was starting to come across as programmed to the eyes with "overarching moral imperatives" and calls to "renew moral fiber." People started to bring up Kennedy's own unfailing compassion, his manifest concern when face to face with human setbacks and weakness.

There had been evidence all along that Romney and his handlers were notoriously thin-skinned. With Kennedy's "$50 million fund," they groused, how could he "stoop to attack" Mitt's earnings? They bellyached when the Kennedy campaign retained Doak, Shrum, Harris, Carrier & Devine, purportedly specialists in negative advertising. Heavy hints were dropped that Ted Kennedy's personal life was up for exploitation if need be, and that the 460-page Republican dossier on Kennedy was available on demand. "He will intentionally try to reverse his brother's victory [over bigotry]," Romney himself announced, "either with self-proclaimed attack dog Joe Kennedy or by himself. . . ." The point was taken — now that it had been made — and Kennedy backed off.

The realization that Kennedy might in fact be well into the process of losing produced a crisis meeting in Kennedy's Back Bay condominium on September 18. Perhaps a dozen of the people closest to the campaign showed up. Vicki's father, Judge Reggie, sat in, while Vicki herself, as always, took full notes.

Michael Kennedy was there, along with pollster Tom Kiley and strategist John Sasso and publicist Bob Shrum. "We got together and we changed fields totally," Shrum acknowledges. "As regards the commitment to the campaign, what we were going to do."

It was already obvious that they would have to pump a lot more money in — estimates were now up from $3 million to $10 million — so that the debate was "not over how much we were going to spend but what we were gong to spend it on. As usual, when responding to difficulty, Kennedy was at his best." The exchanges were heated. "Ted is very different from a lot of people I know in government," Shrum observes. "The quickest way I know to become irrelevant with Ted is to tell him what a great idea he has, or how smart he is.

"We had a couple of testy moments," Shrum remembers. There were inevitably recriminations over having let the television placements slide through July and August. Kennedy finally rounded on Shrum: "'You can be a pain in the ass. I can be a pain in the ass. But my brother Jack always told me, you've got to have a couple of people around who can make real pains in the ass out of themselves.'

"We ran on who Kennedy is," Shrum says. "We never ran away from that. Health care, education, freedom of choice." Shrum also directed media for several other winning Democratic senators — Paul Sarbanes of Delaware, Chuck Robb (much put to the test in Virginia that autumn by Oliver North) — and pushed them too into hardball exchanges which emphasized traditional party positions. Others backed away, especially from health care, and "overall, it wasn't a good year for Democrats."

Nerved up that summer, Kennedy himself got scratchy about the Contract-with-America panaceas Newt Gingrich and his acolytes were hawking. "I mean, the balanced budget amendment will solve all our problems," he broke out at one point. "Term limitations, let's all go to the Cape for the weekend. The death penalty will solve our problem on crime." When aides identified difficulties on which they might capitalize in exchanges with the Republicans, Kennedy insisted on solutions. Nobody cuts the welfare rolls without providing for day care, retraining allowances, housing subsidies. Otherwise, tax breaks today bought social chaos tomorrow.

Budgets closer to home already worried the Kennedy advisors. The ten-plus million dollars the campaign ultimately spent required lots of money the campaign did not have. Moreover, it looked to resources even the candidate didn't have, at least at hand.

The era was decades behind them all when bills for leaflets and advance-men's salaries and hotel vouchers and plane tickets would flood in, and Joseph P. Kennedy would grimace and reach for his checkbook. There once had been a time when, the candidate reelected, the hotel executives and telephone company managers would queue up outside Steve Smith's office in the Pan Am Building. They'd come in one by one, each with his past-due invoice in a folder in his sweaty palm, and Smith would frown — annoyed at being interrupted — and stub his cigarette out, and listen a few restless minutes before looking up to offer the supplicant $.20 on the dollar. Advising him to take it — reimbursement would be dropping any second now to $.10 on the dollar.

Most took it. But Steve was gone. Political vendors had learned. Payment was by credit card, normally cleared in advance.

Kennedy saw this coming, certainly by the spring. As early as the second of June, *Boston Globe* feature writer Sally Jacobs was trailing Kennedy as he roamed the backstairs White House, hunting for a painting his family had presented to the nation years ago, a Monet. "I should have hung onto that thing," Kennedy muttered, perhaps a little ruefully. "Then I wouldn't be worried about raising money for my campaign."

Cash remained on Kennedy's mind. Shortly after his amble through the White House, I got to bantering with Kennedy about a nightmare I'd recently had, during which I found myself elected to public office.

Characteristically, he turned it around. "I feel you might, ah, actually enjoy serving," Kennedy shot back. "The truth is, in my own mind I've often thought of you as a colleague from New Hampshire."

I said I'd think about that, and once I returned home I wrote Kennedy, indicating that I'd pondered what he said and decided to run for senator. I would, however, require a donation of perhaps $20 million to seed my campaign. Since he'd come up with the idea, a cashier's check would suffice.

Kennedy got back within a week. He'd enjoyed our time together, he wrote. Also: "Vicki agrees with me that if you do run for the Senate from New Hampshire we should definitely give you a contribution. In fact, Vicki says if there is anything left in the campaign kitty after my victory, you are welcome to it. Although I'm not sure that $2.99 will be of much help — but it might stake you to a bumper sticker."

By September the shortfall of cash was serious. They'd raised over $8 million, and that was not enough. All along Kennedy bookkeepers had refused to get into the details of trust arrangements within the family. But estimates of Kennedy's estate were shrinking: newspaper projections descended from $50 million to $20 million, and down from there. Kennedy could depend on a taxable cash flow of $500,000 a year, much of it earmarked for office expenses. As advertising bills piled up during the cyclonic weeks before the election, Kennedy took out a second mortgage at Bank of Boston on his house in McLean, Virginia for $2 million.

Kennedy's lawyers now reached an accommodation with Joan Kennedy, going public with assurances to reporters that the much bandied-about $4-5 million settlement of the early eighties was as much as 80 percent too high. Under pressure from all three of her children — who saw the strain under which their father was struggling that fall — Joan dropped her demands for fresh capital in return for provisions in Ted's will to guarantee her income in the event of his death. Nobody in the family had forgotten how strapped Jackie found herself once Jack was murdered, how panics about support money had prompted the Onassis marriage.

Jacking up the ante, Kennedy authorized what local critics characterized as "a virtual miniseries of off-ramp attack ads." Kiley's polls kept showing that Kennedy's favorable/unfavorable ratings lagged Romney's, the warning pattern preliminary to an upset. The problem was — what could they target? Romney himself was young, successful — if not by any means the friendly self-made venture capitalist he presented himself as; Romney's leveraged-buyout maneuvers recalled the previous generation's corporate raiders; Mitt had no cogent political record of his own. His ties to the Republican Party were recent and opportunistic. He admitted quite freely to having voted for Paul Tsongas in the 1992 Democratic primary. The popular Republican governor, William Weld, was leery and reluctant to risk a flank attack on Kennedy in Romney's behalf. Mitt's position on virtually every issue was hard to establish, nebulous — Kennedy himself dismissed Romney's approach to abortion as "multiple-choice."

Once elected, Romney pledged, he would hurry down to Washington to serve as the "jobs candidate." Kennedy was played out, lacked clout, become ineffective. Absurd as this sounded to anybody in touch with business in the Capitol, who understood the ramifications of seniority throughout the Congress, it accorded with the recurrent tabloid fantasy that Kennedy lay bloated in political shallows. Around yuppified Greater Boston there were a good many enclaves where Romney's presentation resonated, his unblemished Stepford-Husband cool roused approval. Here was a man whose handsomely tailored wife, Ann, had divulged that Mitt had not raised his voice to her since the couple were teenagers. This against the tumult of Kennedy's shaggy personal life.

Luck favors the prepared mind. In September of 1994, Kennedy's worried handlers moved. Heavy artillery from everywhere in the Democratic Party, from Paul Tsongas to Jesse Jackson, showed up at fund-raisers to plug The Big Guy. A selection of all-stars from Kennedy's great staffs over the years pitched in. Ranny Cooper enlivened meetings. The incomparable David Burke, just then the beneficiary of successive golden handshakes from CBS News and The Dreyfus Corporation, drove up to travel with Kennedy, his wry basso profundo a talisman to ground the candidate. This could easily amount to the Last Great Battle.

On September 21 Romney breezed through the Republican primary. Kennedy's assault grew serious. One theme that Shrum and his cohorts had started to bedevil was Romney's performance as a businessman, his assertion that Bain had generated ten thousand jobs around the Commonwealth. An outspoken Kennedy ally, Rich Rogers, the AFL-CIO's Massachusetts political director, now publicly dismissed Romney as "just another robber baron. If they look deep enough, they'll find his firm destroyed ten jobs for every job they have allegedly created."

Shrum picked this up. "Romney," an attack ad blazed. "In business he made $11 million in two years while his largest company [Staples] provided no health insurance to many workers. The company pays for it for employees overseas, but not for thousands in the U.S. . . ."

Behind the scenes, a lot of the coordination was coming from Victoria Kennedy, who talked with Shrum every day. Vicki liked to tease Ted by claiming that he only married her to sanitize his image for the upcoming election. That autumn, insiders were beginning to speculate that Kennedy had tied the knot because it was the only way to guarantee for himself Vicki's extraordinary political instincts.

At that point the Kennedy people got a break that hinted of divine intervention. In July a company Bain Capital owned, Ampad, had picked up an affiliate of SCM Office Supplies in Marion, Indiana. Just as their senior management withdrew, the SCM officers laid off the entire paper products plant's work force. Ampad quickly rehired most of the jobless, although in many cases at reduced wages and benefits. As affiliates of the United Paperworkers International Union, the workers went out on strike on September 1.

Robert Shrum's partner, Tad Devine, showed up in Marion with a taping crew days after the strike started. They'd prepared some material, comments the workers could read off a teleprompter into their camcorders. But outrage and despondency at Ampad came through so spontaneously that Devine and his crew tossed aside the script and built their sound bites by zooming in on worker after worker and intercutting and splicing afterward. Immediately after the buyout, one of the jobless maintained, "we had no rights any more." "They cut the wages," another worker asserted, while another chimed in: "We no longer had any insurance, they cut our throats."

Sharon Alter, a "packer" released after twenty-nine years, hammered in the point: "I would like to say to the people of Massachusetts — You think it can't happen to you? Think again, because we thought it wouldn't happen here either."

Heavily aired in early October, these ads made very plain how calculations in the sterility of a Boston boardroom resonated through decent people's lives a thousand miles away. "We'd run the spots," Shrum now recalls, "and naturally we were focus-grouping, rewriting all the time to show, for example, that Senator Kennedy was behind legislation to correct some of these abuses. A spot like that would run for huge points, because it was driving votes like crazy."

Six striking Ampad workers drove east to plead their case in Massachusetts; the local AFL/CIO made sure they appeared on media throughout the state. The fact was, Mitt Romney himself had gone on leave-of-absence months before the Ampad buyout. Nevertheless, he wouldn't really answer the charges. "I'd love to help," he insisted once pickets were in place outside Bain. "But there's a separate management team running the company. I don't work there."

Kennedy's polls picked up. By the end of October the Romney consultants were again on the hunt. They had discovered in a *Boston Herald* flash exposé a remote investment of Joseph P. Kennedy Enterprises in an office building in D.C. Part had been leased to U.S. Government agencies in 1989; Kennedy had been taken out of his .04 percent holding at the time to avoid conflict of interest. Misunderstanding — somebody's calculator needed batteries — Romney launched an ad: "Ted Kennedy. He attacks Mitt Romney's honest record of achievement and makes $10 million for himself at taxpayer's expense." Even Paul Tsongas, never really a Kennedy partisan, was prompt to rebuke the Romney campaign for proceeding on "irresponsible data."

The charge collapsed overnight. Romney moved on immediately to accuse Kennedy of sponsoring judges who were "notoriously pro-criminal." That didn't stick either; such skeptics as Republican consultant John Ellis dismissed the Romney campaign's financial charges as "patently ridiculous. Kennedy knows nothing about money. If his paychecks were lost for four months he wouldn't even know they were missing." Local jurists couldn't deny how picky Kennedy invariably proved with judicial appointments.

After ten months of circling Kennedy, Romney's perception of the incumbent had remained so underinformed and delusional that he was attacking a phantom, meanwhile largely ignoring, for example, such serviceable vulnerabilities as Kennedy's willingness during the previous year to get behind $131 billion in spending measures and only $51 billion in cuts. Campaigning was an expensive way for Mitt to enlighten himself.

While Romney repeatedly reversed himself on abortion and the minimum wage, Kennedy personally remained upbeat. "It isn't just flip-flop, it's flip-flop-flip," he was heard to remark. "If we give him two more weeks, he may even vote for me."

14

By October the obligatory final-stage one-on-one debates between the nominees was almost upon them. Apart from risking a belated sympathy vote, the Romney campaign's months of attempting to present Kennedy as, in the words of *Globe* columnist Bella English, "a tongue-tied, blowzy aging incompetent," with "enough baggage to keep a bellhop busy for life" now rendered the incumbent the underdog. At this point, Kennedy barely needed to show up sober to astonish the hard-core detractors.

After weeks of chivvying each other over the venues and preconditions of the debates, a combined offer from *The Boston Herald* and *The Boston Globe* proved acceptable to both political camps. To prepare himself, Kennedy assembled the familiar suspects at McLean. A former aide, David Smith, played Romney. Shrum served as moderator, while Sasso, Corrigan and Carey Parker doubled for the questioners. Kennedy badgered Smith relentlessly over the details of his health care proposals and teased the others for having negotiated an extra-wide podium to mask Kennedy's bulk.

The initial debate was mounted on Tuesday, October 25, in the historic fastness of Faneuil Hall. "The entire national press corps showed up," Shrum reminisced later. "Everybody was there because they thought Teddy was going to do very badly." Romney operatives had been circulating gibes, embellishing for reporters exactly what their man would do to the incumbent now that "the training wheels will be off."

Through much of the opening exchanges it looked as if the detractors were right. Given the candidates' respective history, Sally Jacobs of the *Globe* demanded of Kennedy, "why is this race even close?" Like almost any life-style question just then, it couldn't help but tilt Kennedy onto the defensive. He immediately looked discomfited, his lips pursed. Conditions were not good, he wanted to emphasize, but with his longevity in the Senate he was in a position to help the state —

Romney cut into that. "Lemme tel ya," he assured the crowd. "This idea of clout gets overstated. Every two years you have a senator who comes here with one of those big cardboard checks. . . ." All that was just more pork, it was past time that "people realize that those checks are drawn on their bank accounts."

Kennedy attempted to rally; his spread jowls, dusted for the occasion with brick-red powder, inflated as he rambled badly in his effort to explain himself, his raddled baritone dropping from time to time in fleeting transports of stage fright.

They proceeded to welfare. Kennedy cited the work-fare legislation that he had overseen through the Senate in the Reagan years, an effort to tighten up the law but not without "a safety net for children. . . ."

Romney brushed that off. "One of the great things about our nation, Sally," he instructed the questioner, and at that moment a sharp ripple of the dismissive preppiness no briefing could expunge came through like a whiff of ammonia. The mood was altering. Few across that audience appreciated this display of scoutmastering.

There was a go-around over abortion; then Kennedy pitched into Romney for boasting about having created those thousands of jobs only to have so many part-time and minimum wage. The Romney modus operandi amounted to closing a plant down, throwing everybody out, then hiring back only the younger workers and dumping the older people. Why not retrain everybody?

As Kennedy and his advisors foresaw, this definitely roused Mitt. "Senator Kennedy and his family have a multiple real estate empire around this country," Romney charged, and in the Merchandise Mart, "the jewel of the empire," the part-time employees did not get health insurance either. Kennedy attempted to mutter something about at the very least providing access. Romney cut him off: "I don't know what you're talking about. You don't supply health insurance."

It was a palpable hit. The exchange moved on, with Romney edging into control. Sally Jacobs had another question. "Senator Kennedy, what is your greatest personal failing?"

This was the sort of query Kennedy detested most, squishy and extremely danger-ridden, but now he made an attempt. He tended to talk about himself, he confessed. Say too much about personal values and personal achievements. And more than that: "I know that I have not lived up to all the expectations of the people of Massachusetts. I have made that statement." But recently, "my life has changed dramatically, I'm trying to be a better father, son, husband. Since my life has changed with Vicki, in personal matters life has been enormously reinvigorating." This was the party line that season, but it was also the truth and obviously it took something out of Kennedy to put himself through even that formulized a mea culpa.

The questioning turned to Romney. His greatest personal failing? Well, Romney opened, as it happened he had given up two and a half years when he was young living with the poor, and even now he spent one day a week "with people less fortunate than myself. . . . I've spent hundreds of hours in hospitals across the state, working with sick people, consoling them —"

The moderator, Ken Bode, finally cut Mitt off: "This was a question about your greatest personal *failing*." The audience broke up.

Romney's failing, it developed, was that he couldn't totally fulfill his "God-given obligations to do more." That he wasn't even more of a saint.

With this the momentum of the evening shifted. In some ineluctable way Kennedy now acquired a centeredness, self-consciousness dropped away, and for the rest of the hour Romney kept jumping at Kennedy, like a suave but too-eager whippet bouncing off a huge old pug. When Romney again attacked Kennedy's "blind trusts" Kennedy stood his ground in solemn tones: "Mr. Romney, the Kennedys are not in public service to make money. We have paid too high a price." That remained in place as Mitt charged that "Marion Barry gave your family a no-bid deal that he wouldn't give to anybody else in this country, and you know it."

They proceeded to health care. Romney attacked the Clinton plan. Kennedy asked him how he would handle the health crisis and Romney cited the Bentsen proposals of the eighties. That wasn't a health proposal, it was an insurance reform package, Kennedy corrected Mitt. He asked after the impact of incentives in a plan like that on the overall budget; Romney snapped that he did not have the "Congressional Budget Office" at his disposal so he could go through the details "piece by piece."

"That's exactly what you have to do with a piece of legislation," Kennedy volunteered with a delicate asperity. For the remaining minutes Kennedy occupied himself pretty largely tutoring his challenger. When Romney lamented the shortage of fathers in mid-city areas, Kennedy admitted that he did not have "a silver bullet" for needs that profound, although he was involved in initiatives to develop families and communities.

"Women!" Romney came back. "Women are concerned about the glass ceiling."

"When I heard that, I thought, 'Well, we've won the debate,'" Bob Shrum recalls. "It was like pitching a slow ball over the plate to Babe Ruth." Kennedy trotted out a range of legislation he had seen through the Congress, from language which helped implement a woman's right to sue on the job to provisions which allocated money to study women's health problems at the National Institute of Health.

As the debate ended, Romney seemed a little out of breath. "C'mon. Folks, c'mon," he kept exclaiming, like somebody being steadily backed off a cliff.

The return engagement at Holyoke Community College two evenings afterward was friendlier, and much, much duller. Within hours of the Tuesday debate the Kennedy campaign had issued a statement specifying that the Merchandise Mart had four hundred employees, seven of whom were part-time. For each it was a second job, and all had health coverage either from other employers, others in their families, or Medicare. That disposed of Romney's bombshell.

The town-meeting format in Holyoke further helped defuse rancor. The podiums in the Holyoke auditorium were small and low, and flanked by very high stools. Kennedy's back was clearly torturing him, and he slumped upright whenever he listened to attempt to ease it a little. His big spongy face looked extraordinarily distended around the jawline, perhaps by medication, and many of his responses were halting — if measured — and laden with forbearance that verged on the lachrymose.

When one of the questioners, a Professor Hamilton, referred to having met the senator in 1962, Kennedy justified those exhaustive briefings: "I remember very well. It was in North Adams, at the Fall Foliage Festival!"

Much of what debate there was revolved around welfare. Here, as again and again throughout the months of the campaign, Romney propounded his breakthrough proposals only to discover that Kennedy had been involved for years in attempts to turn formulations all but identical into law. "I couldn't agree more with the need to take care of our children," Romney found himself concurring at one point. "I couldn't disagree more with his ability to get the job done. He's been there thirty-two years. He knows not only the trees and the forest, he knows the leaves one by one." This came through not so much as a complaint about Kennedy's voting record as a wail of frustration at having to contend with the incumbent's encyclopedic legislative grasp.

Each innovation Romney thought he was introducing, Kennedy shrugged off expertly. Tax breaks for employers who hire welfare recipients? "First of all," Kennedy informed him, "there is already a tax credit on the books. It is not working very well. . . ." To standard Republican bromides like "The best social program is a good job," and "We have to have the jail space to be tougher" on criminals who commit crimes with guns or sell drugs to minors, Kennedy somewhat wearily agreed. Despite Romney's contentions, Kennedy himself had already voted pretty much along the lines Romney suggested, of course. But everybody's experience showed that, especially with teenagers, if you ignore the nourishing of "a sense of self-value and self-worth" and implement merely "a recriminatory system, you're going to fail."

What kept coming through in Kennedy's intricate responses was the social vision of lifetime, an enveloping comprehension of how our multifaceted society operated — and should operate — as the millennium ground out its last few years. This vision undoubtedly owed more than Kennedy himself realized to the continuing Catholic inquiry into what promotes social justice, what individuals owe to and what they should expect from worldly authority. Moving into his sixties, Kennedy shone at moments with reflected light from the City of God.

Obviously aware that Thursday that the ferocity of his lunges at Kennedy during the earlier debate had damaged his numbers, Mitt worked to gentle out his persona. He came over coltish, more affirmative, a kind of rangier Pat Boone. Nothing further was alleged about Kennedy's supposed profiteering. While lean and hungry-looking still, Romney downplayed the bumptious junior executive clambering toward his deal across the bodies piling up. When he attempted to elaborate on the draconian welfare changes he favored he pulled up language from some *Good Housekeeping* glossary that made it all sound domesticated and relatively humane. By legislating according to Kennedy's ideas, he charged at one point, "we'd have kids all over the street, welfare moms at home. . . . If this mom has a problem, I want to get her into rehabilitation." Across the political lawns of Romneyland, "moms" substituted that autumn for the traditional welfare queens.

Occasionally the fangs emerged. When Kennedy put in at one point that he and his family knew enough about crimes and shootings, Romney slammed down ruthlessly: "We heard that before. That's the last resort each time."

Dramatically, the highpoint arrived when one of the questioners, a Cambridge small businessman, asked Kennedy to comment on reports in Rick Burke's memoir that Kennedy had shared cocaine and engaged in sexual harassment of female staffers. Onlookers gasped.

Kennedy seemed more resigned than taken aback. "Well, those are old allegations by a disgruntled ex-employee of mine," he observed, "which were reviewed in their entirety by the Senate Ethics Committee. They are completely false. . . ."

"I don't want your question," Romney quipped when the businessman from Cambridge homed in on him.

During his short summation, Mitt Romney ventured an anecdote. "I was in Dorchester not long ago," he recalled. "Somebody said, 'This is Kennedy country.' I looked around, and I saw boarded-up buildings, and I saw jobs leaving. And I said, 'It looks like it.'"

This was a device Romney would exploit repeatedly during the waning weeks of the campaign. People laughed each time, and each time he undoubtedly lost votes. No politician with sound instincts ventures that close to the outright exclusionary, and Mitt was soon giving away precincts all over the Commonwealth.

Edward Kennedy had started out more vulnerable than he ever appeared before. His accomplished and presentable opponent raised $8 million and spent it without restraint. On November 9 Kennedy won again, 58 percent to 41 percent. He'd seen it coming. "Mr. Romney," Kennedy himself announced just before the end in response to Mitt's characterization of Kennedy country as anywhere in the state troubled by welfare dependency, rising crime, and failing education, "when the votes come in . . . on election night, we're going to board *you* up. We're going to put *you* out of business."

And indeed, they had.

15

I think it was a surprise," Carey Parker will admit, with reference to the overall 1994 elections. Parker is a fixture after going on thirty years around Kennedy's back offices: domey, graying, dry as a Presbyterian deacon at this stage, always intellectually rigorous, so identified with Kennedy after decades of discreet cloakroom negotiations that he is referred to sometimes as the 101st senator. "We really didn't see that Republican tide coming. We were shocked that we lost both the House and the Senate. I think with hindsight it was fairly clear what the Republican strategy had been. . . . Kennedy was, first of all, proud of the campaign he ran, he wasn't giving an inch to, you know, the Republican alternatives on the issues. Other Democratic Senate candidates, including some good friends of Senator Kennedy, felt they had to trim their sails a bit and move toward the middle, toward the Republicans." Accordingly, many lost. "Inevitably," Parker concludes, "the voters will choose the real thing."

I have been visiting these offices for longer than Parker even has been around, and I am reminded each time of how little anything changes. Out in the waiting room a pair of presentation gloves and an admiring note from Muhammad Ali still hang on the wall, quite near a photograph of Joseph P. Kennedy and his three boys who survived the war. The Ambassador stands bristling with self-assurance with the collar of his trench coat snapped up, that case-hardened gull-wing grin fixed for the photographer. Those were exuberant times.

These days a rotation of complacent, pudgy interns, usually male, alternate at the front desk Melody Miller long presided over. What with her golden-blonde tresses and translucent skin and those wonderful Baltic cheekbones, Melody looked to newcomers like some high-fashion mannequin sitting in for an early-morning publicity shoot. This she was not. Whether she was handing out passes to the Senate visitors' gallery or calmly removing the knife with which some heavyset female crazy was about to hurtle by in hopes of scalping the senator, Melody tended the gate those many years with discrimination and serenity. She managed enough conversation with impatient interviewers like me so that we were sometimes secretly sorry when finally our news source meandered out full of apologies to lead us into the back.

Melody has been relocated slightly — as Deputy Press Secretary she spends her afternoons on the telephone, presiding over a media-strewn desk inside while ushering her far-flung clientele of journalists and Kennedy acquaintances to interviews she arranges. As liaison for the world between outsiders and the Kennedy family, Melody has helped pull some fiendishly overheated chestnuts out of a rolling broil of heavy publicity. Her role at times approximates that of Wendy's in a road-show *Peter Pan*. Hers is a devotion money could not buy, ambition will never tincture.

Pretty much the same could be demonstrated of Carey Parker, whose Harvard Law background and Rhodes Scholarship and Ph.D. from the Rockefeller Institute all landed him here, where he is content to help bail out the world in the shadow of his boss. When Parker needed more income than his salary provided, Kennedy found himself another job, his weekly radio badinage with Nevada Senator Alan Simpson; what compensation came in he turned over happily to Carey. Parker tends to bring to the backroom deliberations the mixture of probity and attention to the historical process that David Burke once did; what position papers and speeches he does not write he is likely to edit.

Kennedy does the final revision, often while he awaits his turn to speak, those steel-rimmed glasses sliding a little at a time down the ridges of his nose. He makes the ultimate decisions. "I remember one meeting in 1980," Bob Shrum says, "when we were asked to help figure out whether Ted should run against Carter. It came out four to four. 'The vote is one to nothing,' Kennedy then told us. 'I'm going to run.'"

Parker is often indispensable in framing those decisions. As for the health plan, Parker has determined, "the big mistake was in delaying so long, letting it spill into the campaign year. My own theory is that the Republicans made a rather cynical decision in the spring of '94 that the best way to make major gains in the fall elections was to prevent any significant achievements by President Clinton. Their strategy was, no bill shall pass. They were willing to bring down the temple. Gridlock worked. The Democrats woke up too late."

Thwarted in 1994, Kennedy and the surviving Democrats struggled into 1995. What they woke up to, along with a Republican Congress, was Newt Gingrich and his horde of right-wing-revivalist hoplites in the House and their big-ticket Contract with America. Panic swept the Hill, but "we felt the 1994 election was not in any sense a mandate for the Contract," Parker maintains. "They had the votes to jam it through the House, but then it got to the Senate, and I think Kennedy played a major, major role in developing the arguments about what Republican cuts in medicine would do, what Republican cuts in education would do, the unfairness of the Republican tax plan, which had a superficial appeal to middle-class families but which was heavily weighted against the average person. . . .

"We did a lot in terms of putting together witnesses, held a few forums, since we couldn't hold hearings. Brought in citizens to tell their stories, experts to show the impact that combination of Republican cuts would have on senior citizens, hospitals, public institutions. The press picked it up. They were more than willing to cover the Democratic alternative."

By then the Democrats were starting to regroup. Jim Sasser of Tennessee, who had been expected to replace George Mitchell as Majority — now Minority — Leader, had lost. In the Democratic caucus Kennedy's frolicsome drinking companion, Chris Dodd, went down by a single vote to Tom Daschle of South Dakota, with whom Kennedy quickly fell into a profitable working relationship, pepped up by weekends together in Hyannis Port. The plainspoken Daschle showed plenty of aptitude from the outset at keeping the Democrats focused and together. Relations with the White House held up, especially since the president now found himself largely on the outside and eager for allies in his attempts to deal with a Congress relentlessly generating a continuing flow of "bad legislation coming over from the House," as Parker saw it.

"Dick Riley and Bob Reich in the administration were very receptive. We never had the sense that we were tugging them. We were working very closely with the administration to put together details and data." Before long the nonpartisan — if avowedly illiberal — poll-taker and strategist Dick Morris was on hand to troubleshoot the White House in frantic hopes of bettering the fading president's prospects. Morris constituted "a discouragement" to several of the Kennedyites, with his repeated advice to "triangulate" on policy with Congress. This meant, in effect, to go along with many Republican proposals to shave back entitlement programs and revamp the safety net. "Obviously, he was talking a different, uh, strategy," Parker acknowledges. "But I think it didn't make a lot of difference on the president's final position on these issues." Seasoned White House insiders like ex-Kennedy staffer Harold Ickes, Jr. still exerted considerable drag on Oval Office decision-making. "By the end of 1995, when the Republicans had clearly overplayed their hand, it turned out the country didn't agree. That was the beginning of the end of the Contract with America."

In his matter-of-fact way, what Parker was describing to me highlighted Kennedy's most noteworthy endowment, his instincts as a field commander. Where today's political technicians fixate automatically on numbers, opinion surveys, Kennedy takes in individuals, backgrounds, possible shared interests, the potential for fresh coalitions once the overwrought battlefield clears. While younger colleagues panic — *nobody cares about health issues anymore, focus groups are budget-obsessed* — Kennedy himself has ridden out so many sieges at this point that much of the time the thud of one more Republican battering ram pounds along in concert with his heartbeat. He's endured this many times, this ambuscade of attack ads, the misery of collapsing polls. People's needs don't change. They come back.

Adversity bucks him up. "There was a certain dispiritedness among the Democrats with the loss of the Senate," Carey summarizes, "losing the majority, and I think Kennedy helped pull

all the Senate Democrats out of that by the force of his personality and his leadership. That's his greatest gift."

Melody Miller looked in. It was after six, but both the senator and his staff habitually shoulder on into the evening hours
whenever the Senate is in session. Kennedy was still tied up on
the floor, so we had settled down in his inner office, a vaulting
and shadowy rectangle dominated by John Kennedy's big desk
and a scattering of cherished memorabilia like Rose Kennedy's
framed note upbraiding her youngest for even suggesting that
she got anything less than an A during her schoolgirl days, and
admonishing him for cuss words — she had been dipping into
The Education of Edward Kennedy. Little in the office had altered:
it was still full of serviceable, battered furniture; when I'd
stopped by most recently I spotted Kennedy's Jack Russell ter-
rier, Blarney, gnawing on the leg of a coffee table.

"Nick is back," Melody Miller said. "He can't stay terribly
long, so here is his room when you get done with Carey, 644
Dirksen Building." Melody has a warm, level, businesslike delivery, which, like her pastel blouses and tailored skirts, imparts
a kind of convent-school ebullience and concern with details
to everything she does. Melody never seems completely out of
uniform. She handed me a buckslip with Nick Littlefield's location on it.

"Should I go now?" I said.

"Welllll. I think if you were here another five to seven minutes, and then head over. . . ."

Exactly seven minutes later I shook hands with Carey and
started down the echoing corridor toward one of the big,
brass-trimmed elevators. Now that Ted Kennedy is no longer
the chairman of the Labor and Human Resources Committee
his total staff Capitol-wide has inevitably been trimmed: from
something around one hundred people, Kennedy's payroll

currently numbers fifty-eight, coming back from forty-six. Nobody's found a way to lower the senator's ambition-threshold, however, so what that means is that everybody works twice as hard, the boss in particular. ". . . it seemed like virtually the consistent figure in every task force at every meeting was Ted Kennedy," Tom Daschle commented recently. "He was really like this enthusiastic freshman looking for more work."

Now staff director for the Ranking Minority Member of Labor and Human Resources, Nick Littlefield looked too busy to worry much about their formal drop in status. If Carey Parker ponders legislation from the strategic heights, Nick Littlefield is Kennedy's aide de camp in the hot daily trenches. He relishes the shot and shell. A tallish, knobby shirtsleeved ex-federal prosecutor with a curly bristle of stiff gray hair striping back from his widow's peak and the constricted, overfocused face of the unembarrassed policy wonk, Nick Littlefield spends most of his time six or seven days a week striding around in one of those piled-up satellite suites Kennedy maintains for milling out the legislative paperwork. The work tables are piled up with proposed drafts and outdated press releases; chipped-up battleship-gray file cabinets line the scuffed walls; a houseplant has long since died. The telephone is rarely out of use.

"I don't think Senator Kennedy has *ever* had a better sixteen months in the Senate than since the '94 elections," Littlefield opens flatly. "Because he ran as an outspoken progressive Democrat, fighting for working families, around the issues of jobs, education, health care. That was our mantra during that campaign, and that was what got him reelected.

"People around here were very depressed." Kennedy had stepped forward immediately to "define for the president the role he should play on the two key issues of health and education, that he should not permit one nickel to be cut. Then he put together the whole strategy in the Senate to concentrate on working families."

While Gingrich was marshaling support for nine of the ten measures of the Contract with America through his upstart House of Representatives — only term limits failed — Kennedy and Daschle managed to coalesce the forty-seven surviving Democratic senators as well as a shifting handful of Republicans behind a series of bills and amendments intended to stall Gingrich's momentum. Ignoring a rising chorus of shrill cries from the outraged Right, Kennedy was now embarked on strict class warfare, with emphasis on pointing up abuses and unscrambling the Gingrichian doublespeak intended to camouflage the thrust behind this press of legislation. Measures such as The Taking Back Our Streets Act had been devised to divert federal dollars from crime prevention programs to less costly, more punitive short-term answers. The Job Creation and Wage Enhancement Act bundled a capital-gains tax cut together with a broad-scale effort to "overhaul" — read "weaken" — the government regulatory process.

As Senate Republicans prepared to draft counterpart language, Kennedy let his presence register. He rounded up ninety-six senators behind a bill to close the long-standing legal shortfall which permitted the extravagantly rich to renounce their U.S. citizenship to avoid taxes, the "Benedict Arnold" loophole. He put together a quorum of thirty-four Democratic senators to pay a call on moderate Republican Mark Hatfield, chairman of the Appropriations Committee, to advise Hatfield that if the anticipated additional billion were stripped from the pending education bill to satisfy the House in conference, legislators could count on a presidential veto. By July 5 articles were appearing in editorial columns around the country under Edward Kennedy's name which identified Republican initiatives "built around lavish tax cuts that primarily benefit the wealthy," already projected at $245 billion, while Medicare budgeting was down $180 billion. Kennedy forged the linkage in the public's mind.

"We made this chart," Littlefield explained to me, dragging it out from behind something and propping it up. It itemized Republican efforts to slash Wages, Medicare, College Opportunities and Education.

With Gingrich wheeling siege machinery into place, "We'd bring that chart down to the Senate floor every Friday afternoon," Littlefield says. "He'd talk for two hours about that stuff. It just picked up momentum. Every time we had a chance we organized amendments around those four issues.

"Whether it was minimum wage or Davis-Bacon or student loans or Medicare or nursing home standards or pensions — these were all Kennedy's issues. We were on the floor when there were opportunities to organize votes, we organized a whole strategy around the recision bill, around restoring education funding. And Kennedy was constantly beating the drum for taking a stand on Medicare, which was the issue which was really getting through to the public."

Off the Senate floor, Kennedy visited all over town. As early as December of 1994 he'd closeted himself with Clinton before a presidential radio address, urging him to dig in publicly against the proposed rise in Medicare premiums and the expected round of education cuts. "He was at the White House five or six times," Littlefield remembers, "talking to the president about holding the line, sending memoranda, talking with Gore, Ickes, Stephanopoulos. He kept after Vic Fazio, Gephardt, David Bonior in the House. And at the same time, when he found a Republican like Jefford or Campbell who seemed sympathetic on issues like education he kept after *them,* sometimes on the phone. Last week we were able to restore the three million dollars to education funding, and we won it by six votes."

By bundling so many purported changes into each plank of the Contract, the Republicans tempted Kennedy and his experts across unexplored frontiers of lawmaking. "The Republicans were always trying for what they called regulatory reform," Littlefield continued. Much of the intent was obfuscated in impenetrable formulations, so "We were always trying to simplify what the Republicans were all about, find some straightforward, easily understandable consequences of what they were up to."

Littlefield broke into a sudden fierce shy grin as he turned over another chart, white letters on faded blue. "What they called the Regulatory Reform Bill, we called The Polluters and Poisoners Protection Act. It seemed to mandate 'unsafe drinking water, unsafe meat, unsafe fruits and vegetables, unsafe baby food.' Meat would be polluted with E. coli bacteria, fruits and vegetables would have cancer-causing pesticides on them if the Republicans managed to remove safety standards. Kennedy made a whole crusade out of this."

Another Gingrich initiative which Kennedy managed to short-circuit in the Senate was the recurrent proposal to take hundreds of thousands of mothers off welfare while allocating virtually nothing for child care. "We called it the 'Home Alone Bill," Littlefield says. He chuckles. "We created a big problem for Dole around that. Dole put some more child care money in, which we lost in the House."

Nick had to interrupt the interview to take a call from Kennedy himself. It was approaching 7 P.M. That week — late March of 1996 — Kennedy had an amendment in the works to raise the minimum wage. "Well, we've got all the groups ginned up," Littlefield told his boss. "We have to decide what we're going to do. About the workup. We can't object until two hours after he comes in, so that means 11:30. I'll take it to the floor staff in the meanwhile. Yes, well, thanks to your parliamentary experience. I worked the room, and everybody wrote their stories after your press conference. Right. In any event, I'll see you at a quarter of eight."

Littlefield hung up. Even half of the conversation attests to what a three-dimensional chess game lawmaking can be, how moves on every level can advance or stymie a program. "Here we are on the day Dole clinched the nomination for himself in California," Littlefield burst out, exhilarated, "and Kennedy has outsmarted Dole and gotten the minimum wage amendment onto the floor. Right now Dole is so scared of the issue he's going to have to recess the Senate rather than risk a vote!"

Littlefield is so sharp, so ready with statistics and answers, that Kennedy takes a particular delight in catching him on the uptake. "That's in the briefing sheet — I'm surprised you didn't pick that up, Nick," he chided his hard-driving aide recently at an early-morning skull session with a clutch of experts. "Page three!" When Littlefield cuts across the ruminations of one of the consultants, Kennedy wastes no time: "Will you let him talk, Nick!" Another overscheduled day was on them all, and Kennedy was already edgy.

So much of Kennedy's time that winter went into containing Republican brainstorms. The effort was afoot to raise $4.4 billion by charging colleges and universities fees in connection with the federal loans they administer. Kennedy stepped on consideration of a measure to permit private companies to tap employee pension funds. ("This is one cookie jar," he was quoted at the time, "that Republican hands are not going to get into.") Republican budgeteers nourished proposals to foreclose on private residences to pay back Medicaid for nursing-home expenses for the elderly, then billing out the surviving heirs for additional charges. Kennedy disposed of that.

By April of 1996 eight of the nine Democratic bills that Minority Leader Thomas Daschle identified as "priority legislation" came directly out of Kennedy's shop. What one year before had seemed an irresistible Gingrich juggernaut had largely fallen apart, shattered by a long winter of presidential vetoes of the wish-list budgets the Republicans seemed willing to bankrupt the government over. Vetoes, and a primarily Kennedy-led counterattack in the Senate that left the Contract mired down in intra-party Republican factionalism exacerbated by heavier and heavier national coverage.

At that point, Kennedy was thinking positive. With the Republican takeover, Nancy Landon Kassebaum replaced Kennedy as chairman of the wide-ranging Labor and Human Resources Committee. A considerate and reasonable woman, Kassebaum's Senate colleagues have generally appreciated her as a person, and Kennedy has certainly taken pains over the years to accord her an extra measure of courtliness and warmth. There have been policy differences: Kassebaum has been adamant in her determination to scale back OSHA and reduce governmental involvement with student loans, and was a principal proponent for loading administrative charges on universities which accepted public support.

Despite the Democratic minority on the committee, Kennedy has been adroit enough at inside politics to frustrate Kassebaum's revisionist preferences. Where they have agreed, they've several times converted almost the entire Senate. After months of preparation overseen by a young one-time Dukakis and Weld administration consultant, Stephen Spinner, Kennedy and Kassebaum came to agreement on a bill that consolidated dozens of worker training programs, raised grant levels, and shifted implementation largely out of Washington. By October of 1995, the draft was in place and Spinner was dying at thirty-four of cancer. Two days before he died Kennedy showed up at Stephen's home in Cambridge to hash over last-minute plans for the floor debate. The bill passed the Senate 95-2. Kassebaum stood up on the floor immediately after the passage of the bill to broach a testimonial to Spinner's contribution, and broke down. Not much steadier, Kennedy rose to round out the tribute, which he confessed to sharing with her "heart and soul."

By then Edward Kennedy and Nancy Kassebaum were polishing up the health bill which already bore their names. The finished legislation guaranteed access to insurance to all who lost or left their jobs or suffered from preexisting medical conditions. It forbade insurance companies from denying coverage to employers based on the health status of individual employees. It made the cost of long-term health care deductible and increased the health-care deduction for the self-employed.

The response at both political extremes was predictable. Labor tended to dismiss the impact as ameliorative, largely a portability Band-Aid. Conservative ex-governor of Delaware Pete DuPont called it "socialized medicine by the back door."

On April 23, 1996 the Kennedy-Kassebaum health bill passed the Senate 100-0. Kennedy beat back a Dole-sponsored amendment to include "medical savings accounts" for the carriage trade, an up to $4,000 tax deduction against high-deductibility coverage. "For him to pick up the pieces like that is typical of Kennedy," Jack Farrell notes. "Build what you can, then nudge, nudge, nudge. With Kennedy, it's the steps that you take. Kennedy-Kassebaum shows that he's as wily and crafty as ever with half the staff and none of the priorities the chairman can hold in the Senate."

This was a crowning success for Kennedy — potentially. A counterpart version was debated in the House, where, more than Kennedy's, Kassebaum's conciliatory tendencies kept Gingrich's Young Turks suspicious. "In a lot of ways, Orrin Hatch was easier to deal with when he was chairman of the Health Committee," one insider states frankly. "He was a strong, savvy legislator in his own right, he followed through and got things done. Other conservatives trusted him.

"Kassebaum is more of a moderate. The deals have a way of slipping away from you. We'd had this incredible six years, and now since Kassebaum became the chairman not one bill enacted through this committee has made it into the laws. It's because she can't get along with the Republicans in the House. Kennedy has tried to help: he's resisted the more extreme proposals that have come through, especially in the labor area."

Nick Littlefield echoes a lot of this. Accompanying me out, he starts to dream aloud, a devout tactician's reverie: "Long term, it may turn out that the failure of the Clinton health care bill ushered in the Republican landslide of 1994, and that landslide unleashed such extreme forces that it has turned the country against Republicanism for a generation and regalvanized the Democratic majority. Then this year many of the extreme Republicans would lose, and many of the conservative Democrats will retire.

"If that happens," Littlefield says, his intense visionary's eyes taking on light from the corridor, "then the last laugh on health care belongs to Kennedy, and we'll get it done next time."

———

While the 1996 elections were not to repudiate the two-party system in America, what did register was the determination of the voters not to relinquish the security of sixty years of remedial social legislation in exchange for some Republican spinmaster's slogan of the moment. Gingrichism imploded. What transfused both parties as their representatives returned to pick up their desks in Washington was a morning-after sobriety about the real issues — the need to deal with the deficit, public demand for Medicare and Medicaid, an awareness that health care was going to get more expensive every quarter, and no kind of quick fix or profusion of sound bites or rejiggering in the private sector could hope for long to contain the crisis. By acknowledging this, legislators of every orientation now found themselves under pressure to confront the real problems across the health and human welfare spectrum — the place from which Kennedy had been operating for decades. With realism setting in, Nick Littlefield might yet prove right.

16

Politics is largely timing. At the end of April 1996, Edward Kennedy was clinking champagne glasses all over Washington after having somehow convinced all ninety-nine of his colleagues to get behind the landmark Kennedy-Kassebaum Health Insurance Reform Bill. Six weeks later, alarmed that Bob Dole manifestly intended to ignore the recommendations of the Democratic leadership and pack the delegation to the conference committee with the House with members amenable to medical savings accounts, Kennedy was backtracking fast to nullify his triumph. This tax break could only drive up premiums for the sick and needy. Kennedy was openly prepared, and nobody was questioning it, to invoke his prerogative and hold out for as many as ten separate votes while the Senate leadership haggled over selection of the conferees. This process could jam the consideration of anything else for weeks. It was an election year; senators needed to get home to campaign. The Kennedy-Kassebaum bill was side-tracked.

Politics, like Ireland, is a sow that eats its own farrow. Kennedy's thinking was plain enough. Staff around the White House had indicated that the president would very likely veto any health legislation adulterated with "the killer amendment" — medical savings accounts. Quite possibly, he would. And if the House were to return with a Democratic majority in November, and possibly the Senate too, who could really tell what all-encompassing medical reforms might open up overnight? There were clearly risks, but politics is risky, and when had that ever dismayed Kennedy?

Dick Armey and other hard-right ideologues in the House sometimes attempted to vilify Kennedy for stepping on his own bill, but beyond that it was surprising overall how little heat he took. Both polls and focus groups indicated widespread revulsion with Gingrich. It turned out Medicare really *was* the third rail of American politics. Ted Kennedy, on the other hand, seemed to have taken on that peculiarly American sanctity that devolves on a reformed sinner. Even the ever-innovative Richard Viguerie, fund-raiser to the Right, found receipts falling off sharply whenever he tried to resurrect Kennedy to his time-honored prominence as bogeyman from the Left. A consensus was forming among scholars of the Senate that, as Ross Baker of Rutgers put it, "It's not just occupying a seat — but to have had an influence to varying degrees on important aspects of public policy over nearly forty years ranks with the Henry Clays and Daniel Websters."

In January of 1995 another death bump had bounced Kennedy back into the news. Rose Kennedy died at 104. Until she was wheelchair-ridden by strokes a decade earlier, Rose had continued the regimen of travel and self-discipline that kept her lively and competent if, ultimately, remote within her family as the generations proliferated. Obituaries described her in later years as "carrying her own clubs, played nine holes of golf alone against the biting gusts of sea air" of the autumn Cape. "Mother would have been a great featherweight," her surviving son observed. "She had a mean right hand."

Ted was especially devoted. "After his mother became infirm," a family friend remembers, "the first thing he would do at Hyannis Port was put down his briefcase and go to her room. You'd hear his booming voice: *Hello, Muthah, we're here for the weekend.* And every week he would show her clips and video tapes of what he was doing. They'd bring a priest in and Ted would serve the mass in the living room. Sometimes somebody would play the piano and they would sing Irish songs and Ted would say things like: "Do you remember, Mother, how Agnes would enjoy this?"

On better days, Kennedy would insist on pushing his mother's wheelchair out onto the beach, he none too steady and she somewhat crumpled to one side and heavily bundled up. Rose was, at best, marginally in and out. There were occasionally moments. She was 102, Kennedy reports, when he stopped by her room just before a tennis match. "So that's where my tennis racket went!" he says she teased him as he loomed in the doorway. "I've been wondering."

Rose Kennedy was laid to rest beside Joe in Brookline. She left behind forty-one great-grandchildren.

Two were Ted's grandchildren. One girl, Grace, was born to Kara, who emerged from a bumpy adolescence to put in time helping run a family philanthropy called Media for the Very Special Arts, a provider of cultural outlets to the mentally challenged, as the phrase goes. Her husband, Michael Allen, is an architect who specializes in historic restorations.

Another grandchild, Kiley, also a girl, appeared within a month of Kara's to her sister-in-law, Kiki, Teddy Jr.'s wife. Kiki is a psychiatrist who teaches at the Yale Medical School, where the expansive Teddy for some years directed the Welch Center, which identifies and detoxifies children contaminated with lead based paint. Teddy, Jr. is currently finishing law school.

Most unexpected to Kennedy watchers was probably the career turn Ted's youngest took. After recuperating from the perilous operation to remove a growth from his spinal cord, the shy and rather reflective Patrick informed his father that he had decided on a commitment to politics. While still in college in Providence he ran for the Rhode Island legislature at twenty-one and took his seat after expending a record $93,000, $78 per vote. Although Patrick's asthma-threatened personal manner suggested that he must struggle with himself to push a word in edgewise, he developed a reputation for persistence and integrity — especially on the labor issues, as he began showing up on picket lines throughout the little state — and worked out his own stands irrespective of the party bosses. Finishing out six terms, he emerged as chairman of the Rules Committee.

In 1994 he ran for the U.S. Congress from Rhode Island's First District. Even in his mid-twenties, Patrick Kennedy, while tall, what with his big unblinking eyes and English public-school bowl-cut, came over as a kind of throwback, perhaps to the fifties, the sort of novice in a suit and tie who rang your doorbell and pressed a copy of *The Watchtower* into your palm while stammering through his pitch.

In crumbling old Providence, Patrick beat his primary opponent, a convicted sex offender, and proceeded into an extremely nasty campaign against the Republican nominee, Dr. Kevin Vigilante. Both campaigns were heavily financed — Patrick raised and spent just over $1 million, and Vigilante approximately $800,000. An idealistic if somewhat impulsive ex-football player whose forthrightness was the despair of his handlers, Vigilante soon found himself trading virulent attack ads with the experienced Kennedy operatives. Kennedy accused Vigilante of accepting money from the National Rifle Association; not true, Vigilante claimed, but the attacks continued. Kennedy accused Vigilante of not merely underwriting a new car but also of putting himself through medical school on the proceeds of a lawsuit against an elderly Providence woman as the result of a traffic accident in oldster-heavy Rhode Island. "He sued his way for his education," Patrick told the media. But Vigilante was up and about now. "Maybe he found a miracle cure."

Lagging in the polls, the increasingly agitated doctor lashed out at his assailant in JFK Plaza: "In the real world, if I had been an alleged witness to an alleged sexual assault committed by my cousin, ran from the press, denied any knowledge — only to admit that I *did* have knowledge — I could not be a credible material witness. In the real world, if I broke the law by using cocaine, I could not have actually considered running just two years later to become a lawmaker for the state."

But this was not the real world, at least that summer. Caroline Kennedy flew in by private jet to pump for her cousin; Tony Bennett bobbed up to soft-shoe through a fundraiser.

The last few weeks, while Kevin Vigilante finished out his schedule of greeting and handshaking with two fingers pressed against the bridge of his nose to keep the pain of losing under control, he mounted a final $50,000 flurry of ads which featured the eighty-four-year-old landlady for Patrick's campaign, who asserted that the pleasant-spoken young scion had stiffed her for $3,400 in rent. And without any apology, despite all the spaghetti she had sent downstairs from her flat throughout the critical months.

That did help some, if not nearly enough. Patrick won by 54-46. He proceeded to Washington, already warding off death threats, prepared, like his father, to become "a work horse, not a show horse," while undertaking "the daily grunt work of public service." He had foresightedly memorized the names and faces of all 434 colleagues. Patrick, at twenty-seven, would be the youngest member seated.

Patrick makes his way across the Hill from time to time to offer his father the pleasure of counseling him for an hour or so over lunch in his office. Generally they vote alike, although Patrick is likely to vote somewhat more conservatively on social issues. He joined the majority, for example, in opposing the partial birth abortion. He fell in line behind the B-2 bomber. Ted loves to tease him. "Don't tell me you counted the Republican ballots too!" he remembers chiding Patrick when his son put time in tallying the vote count in one of the Rhode Island bi-elections.

Both houses were chafing to adjourn by early August of 1996 — the prospect of returning to the hustings for the August break as majority members of the "do-nothing 104th Congress" was starting to panic the Gingrich Republicans. By then Kennedy's delaying tactics with the health bill, capped by several days of subcommittee maneuvering to tighten the regulations on insurance companies during job changeovers, yielded up the bill he was after all along. Gaining momentum from the broad-scale welfare revisions passed the previous week — which Kennedy expressly hated — the Congress on August 2 rushed through the updated Safe Water Drinking Act, the long-sought legislation to raise the minimum wage by $.90 over the next two years, and a perfected version of the Kennedy-Kassebaum bill that contained no more than a "pilot program" experiment with medical savings accounts.

Summoned later that day to appear on *The Newshour with Jim Lehrer,* both Kennedy and Nancy Kassebaum emphasized that their bill addressed only a few of the most urgent problems in our ramshackle health-care system. But, later in the broadcast, pundit E. J. Dionne of *The New York Times* summed up the outcome of two years' control in both houses of Congress by insurgent right-wingers: "This is not the Republican Contract with America, it's Ted Kennedy's Contract with America." Falling back on persistence, salesmanship, and unmatched parliamentary legerdemain, Kennedy had again helped turn the entire flank of American lawmaking.

With the health insurance bill pending, Kennedy decided the winter of 1996 to reconnoiter a new front. The debates with Romney had reminded Kennedy that many of the deepening problems in post–Cold-War America traced back to favoritism in the tax laws, the infiltration by generations of lobbyists and special-interest conservatives from both parties of what was now starting to go by the name "corporate welfare."

This wasn't a new issue, and took some resonance in Kennedy's touchy family from over a century of agreement that, as JFK once quoted his father, "most businessmen are sons of bitches." The emergence of multinational corporations had intensified the surreptitious recasting of the tax code, increasingly to the detriment of what was left after the Reagan onslaught of organized labor and unaffiliated working people. As factory employment waned in favor of service positions, and jobs moved overseas, ripples reached national politics. By the middle nineties, the phenomenon agitating stump speakers in both parties was the steadily falling spendable incomes of regular working Americans.

As a Democratic Advisory Council founder, Bill Clinton kept attempting to straddle this discomfiting issue. After an extended delay, Kennedy himself had gone along with Clinton and voted for U.S. entry into NAFTA and GATT, both condemned by longstanding Kennedy allies like Steve Early of the Communications Workers of America for endangering millions of Stateside jobs while making it harder and harder to keep the international corporations answerable. From home-grown militia hotheads to disgruntled John Birchers, the awareness was spreading that wealth was polarizing society, that indulgence of the international corporations was speeding this disastrous process up. The success of Pat Buchanan's scathing neo-isolationism throughout two cycles of Republican primaries attested to the issue's potency.

Typically, Kennedy abstained from the perennial the-rich-are-killing-us shibboleths of the shopworn Left and set his people to dissecting the intricacies of the tax code itself. Kennedy wanted a comprehensive analysis, and then he wanted remedies. Experts and specialists flew in for early-morning brainstorming sessions at McLean. Kennedy added to his staff a prominent New York attorney who specialized in international law, Dennis Kelleher. On February 8, 1996, Kennedy sounded fair warning in a speech at the Center for National Policy in Washington entitled "The Rising Tide Must Lift More Boats."

He summarized the problem: "President Kennedy said that a rising tide lifts all boats," Kennedy asserted, "And for the golden decades after World War II, that was true. But today's rising tide is lifting only some of the boats — primarily the yachts." While productivity was rising, real wages were sinking. Corporations laid workers off even in good times. Parents were forced to work several jobs, to the detriment of their children. "A storm is coming, and the effects are already being felt by most families."

In fact, the Government itself seemed to be colluding in this socially catastrophic process. The Federal Reserve Board, fixated on throttling down inflation, was choking off growth. Kennedy proposed certain remedies. Initiate a new corporate tax rate which rewards companies which create better-quality, higher-paying jobs at home. Such companies should receive better capital gains treatment for their investors as well as preferential treatment when government contracts are awarded. To fund these incentives, Kennedy proposed "eliminating costly tax loopholes that encourage layoffs, discourage job creation, and reward companies for moving American jobs overseas. Over the next seven years, corporate welfare, tax loopholes and tax preferences will cost the federal government over four trillion dollars. In 2002, these tax entitlements will represent a far larger share of the federal budget than Social Security, Medicare, or Medicaid."

Pointing out that in 1991, for example, 73 percent of foreign-based businesses and over 60 percent of U.S. companies paid no U.S. income taxes, Kennedy pinpointed the abuses which contributed to this hemorrhage of revenue:

The "transfer-pricing loophole," through which multinationals avoid taxes by "shifting income through rigged transactions to overseas subsidiaries."

The "runaway plant loophole," which permits foreign subsidiaries of U.S. companies to defer taxes on income earned abroad, profits which are ultimately sheltered once they are invested overseas. "The painful, preposterous result is that our tax laws generate new jobs and investments in foreign countries rather than here at home in America."

The "foreign sales corporation loophole, a paper shell that lets companies shield 30 percent of their income from U.S. taxes."

The "title passage loophole," which allowed companies to claim that U.S. sales were made on foreign soil, so they could be offset by foreign tax credits.

The "Benedict Arnold loophole," which permits "billionaires to renounce their citizenship and move to a foreign tax haven...."

Even before his speech, Kennedy had been field-testing these tax reforms where he saw openings around the government. At a freewheeling powwow with the leadership in both parties in mid-December of 1995, just as the federal government itself was sliding off-budget, President Clinton personally appeared to be intrigued by Kennedy's exhortations to shut the corporate loopholes down, his demonstrations that "There is real feeding at the trough." The president asked that details be sent to the White House directly. But throughout the hours Kennedy was lobbying his case, aides to Treasury Secretary Robert Rubin and Chair of the Economic Council Laura Tyson continued to work the room.

"They don't want to do it because they basically are a spokesman for many of these industries," Kennedy grumped to an interviewer. "I would like Bob Rubin to tell me the best ones to cut. I would like him to tell me, and tell the president, how to do it. But he is representing a different kind of constituency. He knows it. I know it. The president sort of knows it. So that makes it a political issue."

This was a rare, unguarded breakout of Kennedy's suppressed impatience with the divided administration. Like much of the Democratic leadership, Kennedy was put off by the president's penchant for going soft around the edges whenever principle threatened to collide with politics. Clinton could wobble badly that close to the fall elections. Particularly galling was the president's widely telegraphed readiness to sign the "Personal Responsibility and Work Opportunity Act of 1996," the Orwellian title its Republican sponsors attached to the welfare reform legislation.

The welfare revisions Clinton had been promoting since 1992 would have cranked up the overall cost of welfare in America by ten billion dollars a year to provide the day care and job training recipients were expected to require. The bill he signed carved $56 billion from existing expenditure levels, with some of what was left having been earmarked, if not very precisely, for vocational and child care purposes as part of the block grant distribution to the states. An additional 1.1 million children were expected to grow up now in unrelieved poverty.

Kennedy let himself be quoted the day the welfare changes went into law as baffled by this "let-'em-eat-cake" approach. The extent of his disillusion crept into his February 1996 speech on corporate welfare. After flogging a wide range of administrative changes, from extending the antitrust laws to restricting new combinations which promote layoffs to better protecting unions and subsidizing additional research and development and simplifying regulatory procedures, Kennedy squared off directly to confront a number of the issues which were bulking up the Buchanan campaign.

We should, Kennedy announced, "do more to defend American workers against low-wage labor and sweatshop practices from overseas. It is not protectionist to refuse to compete on the basis of who can exploit their workers the most. We should declare a pause before entering into new free trade agreements, so our economy and our companies can adjust to NAFTA and GATT. . . ."

What had been going around was finally coming around. From the trickle-down theoreticians of Herbert Hoover to Ronald Reagan's supply-side deficit dervishes to exponents of the post-industrial tomorrow which reflected the New World Order, a lot of common economic sense had been out on holiday. A concern for ordinary working Americans had given way to the self-interest of the power elite. From time to time, Kennedy himself bought in. Listeners discerned a note of remorse when it came to Kennedy's eleventh-hour support for NAFTA.

Whatever the customary assurances, each phase in implementing the treaty had led us deeper into economic quagmires. Despite months of administration insistence that it would hold out for better labor conditions and environmental protections beyond the Rio Grande, in short order NAFTA had produced a collapsed peso, a tremendous loan to the Mexicans to bail out Robert Rubin's friends among the American lenders, a vast trade deficit with Mexico where recently had been a surplus, devastation of the Mexican economy, and the disappearance of what was estimated to amount to a million American jobs, many thousands in agriculture. Perot's Giant Sucking Sound was audible again, and closing.

Kennedy's February 1996 speech had cast a long shadow up Pennsylvania Avenue, one guaranteed to reach the White House. It hinted of enormous upcoming agendas. He had as ever carefully positioned himself. The fight was on for Bill Clinton's ephemeral soul.

The stakes were rising again; nevertheless, Kennedy continued to work both sides of the aisle. Although Congress remained trapped in partisan deadlock, Kennedy managed to coauthor a bill with Bob Dole to authorize a Whaling Park in New Bedford in return for the Nicodemus Historical Site in Kansas. He shamed the majority into supporting a disclosure bill on prescription pharmaceuticals opposed by the drug industry, and cosponsored with arch-conservative Lauch Faircloth successful church arson legislation. Meanwhile, Kennedy protected the high-tech handouts and research grants on which so many Massachusetts corporations battened.

Yet little by little, for all his bipartisan footwork, Kennedy was increasingly aware that a historic crisis was coming. That two Republican parties, as he sometimes joked, was one, at least, too many. That unless deep-seated reforms were instituted, and soon, the game was likely to break up once and for all.

17

M uch as he likes the president personally, Kennedy has recognized all along where principal gave way to panicking toward the advantage of the moment around the Clinton White House. "Disillusioned?" one of Kennedy's lieutenants responded to me soon after the election of 1996. "It was always hard to be illusioned. You have to retain the sense that this is somebody who is powerful and effective politically. He represents a chance to get things done. You don't do it with a Panglossian vision of Clinton as a person. You play smart political ball."

Smart and — behind the scenes — at times very tough. "Clinton was made aware," the Kennedy operative continues, "when the budget deal was pending in 1995, and Dick Morris was pushing Clinton to compromise on Medicare with the Republicans, that he wasn't only going to face a lot of open opposition from Senator Kennedy and Dick Gephardt, but that he might well have confronted a primary challenge. That's what his deputy chief of staff Harold Ickes was arguing at the time — it wasn't a set of political maneuvers but rather policy preferences that were going to save the presidency. Clinton didn't really want to make that fight, but then there's always been that problem. . . ."

Kennedy himself campaigned hard around the country, for both the president and an assortment of local candidates. Most urgent had been the reelection of John Kerry in Massachusetts. Kerry's campaign floundered badly the summer of 1996. His opponent, Massachusetts Governor William Weld, managed to sell the voters of the Commonwealth on the proposition that he really wasn't that Republican on the social issues — he was demonstrably pro-choice, he favored gay rights, etc. But Kerry was unreliable on crime, welfare, and taxes, and that was the real difference between them.

With Kerry's numbers collapsing, Kennedy got increasingly worried and convinced his colleague that the single most important thing he could do was to let in a number of Kennedy's own key people to refocus the campaign. Bob Shrum took charge of the media for the duration, and Kennedy technicians like John Giesser were detached from the Clinton-Gore campaign. Charlie Baker came back for the critical later weeks and helped Kerry background himself for the interminable series of public debates with Weld which ran almost until election day. Television spots and the substance of the argument between the candidates were moved inexorably back toward traditional Democratic issues — health, Medicare, education, the environment, minimum wage. John Kerry came back day by day and, in the end, won handily.

The standoff the elections provided left Kennedy and his people circling cautiously to await Clinton's second term. There was a lot of concern about Harold Ickes's bumpy exit from the administration, along with the wholesale resignations of left-leaning senior staffers like George Stephanopoulos and

Leon Panetta. The ascent of the efficient, pro-business Erskine Bowles to chief of staff had not reassured the Kennedy brain trust. "There's some sort of fight going on for the president's soul and prerogatives," one of them assured me after Ickes was bounced. "The president himself has signaled his own sort of indecision. One day he says he's for the balanced budget amendment, the next day he has his people calling around to say he's not. He's having trouble deciding on the cabinet. Clinton now has a chance to make a difference. But we don't know yet what difference it will be."

Inevitably, there were long second thoughts about the campaign itself. "Once all the revelations about John Huang and all the Indonesian money broke, you did see a lot of deflation in the president's numbers," Bob Shrum told me not long before Thanksgiving. "Without that, over the last ten days or two weeks of the campaign Clinton would have gotten 53 or 54 percent of the vote. The difference is, that margin would have produced a Democratic House and probably a few more Senate victories." With gridlock again threatening, "Clinton's second term remains unformed. The Republicans keep sending signals back that basically say, 'Sure, we'll be bipartisan, send us something. C'mon, send us something.' Then, when he sends it, they're going to punch him in the nose.

"The hope is — I know Senator Kennedy's hope is — that the president will wake up some morning soon and realize that this is a transformational time for him. He isn't going to have another election. He's either going to pass things he cares about, or not pass things he cares about. And so he better be careful that what he sends is really something he wants to fight for."

By December 12, when I caught up with Kennedy for the last time, his normal wary hopefulness seemed pitted as much by concerns about the second-term Clinton agenda as about the carryover Republican majority in Congress. "There's no question but that the budget squeeze, in terms of trying to reach a balanced budget in five years, is going to be much more serious this year than last, yes," he agreed when I referred to the resignations of Ickes and Stephanopoulos and Panetta.

This was an administration of bookkeepers, his heavy forbearance suggested, and Kennedy referred to the recent testimony of Felix Rohatyn and Bernie Schwarz of Loral, who both emphasized that the United States was now carrying the lowest percentage of debt compared with its Gross National Product in the industrial world. "If all we do in the next two years is just debate whether we're five years out or seven years out in terms of a balanced budget, well, that's not a very productive use of the time or talents of this Congress."

There might be $80 billion in new revenue the first year if Congress got serious about corporate welfare reform, Kennedy conjectured, and $35 billion and rising a year after that, and for some reason Congress gave the Pentagon $12 billion last year it hadn't even requested. So money was out there. Meanwhile, "What has been developing in America since 1972 is an enormous disparity, with close to 65 percent of Americans losing ground. So that's the overarching issue as we go into the next century." Kennedy summed it up: "Is the system going to work for a few, or should it work for everybody? It's clear to me that we're just going to have to pull and haul in terms of the priorities."

You're talking about the White House end of Pennsylvania Avenue? I put in.

"Well." There was a pause. "We might. I did it last year on welfare, and I did it last year on habeas corpus — you know, the anti-terrorist bill. We're prepared to work with them all that we can, but I'm prepared at times I think that programs are wrong to . . . to vote no."

"And do you think you're going to get a majority of the Democrats to go along with you?"

"Well, we did last time," Kennedy reminded me. "You know, historically, the Democrats have been the representatives of the public interest. And the others have been the protector and projector of the special, more narrow interests. All along there's been this tension between the role of the corporation as a wealth generator and its responsibility to society. We're basically the empowerment party, we believe in empowering people in terms of bettering education, health, jobs in the economy, a greater sense of optimism. Programs come and go, but values don't. I'm a believer in that."

The shade of Hubert H. Humphrey rose behind us as we spoke. On up days, somebody close to Kennedy had recently tipped me off, there were again intimations that he might just go for the presidency in 2000. Carey Parker went along to the convention in Chicago last summer with express orders to butter up the delegates. That could be serious, or possibly a feint for leverage with the returning administration. Either way, by now Bill Clinton should recognize fair warning.

"I suppose in time even those great Kennedy genes tend to start winding down," remarked one cynic from the press when asked about Ted's extracurricular activities of late. Where lights are brightest — and dimmest — nobody has seen him recently.

The stories one does hear cleave to the domestic. A magnet for youngsters, Kennedy keeps things interesting at McLean by competing with his stepchildren, Curran and Caroline, to see who can hold out the longest standing on his/her hands upside down in the pool. Even when the Senate is in session all but around the clock, Kennedy slips out for dinner at home when Vicki is working late and deals with his share of the carpooling and game attending. One seasoned White House operative during the later seventies, who long had shared the Carter staff's disdain for Kennedy after several years of bitter skirmishes, called up an acquaintance from Ted's entourage to admit, finally: "OK, you win, I really like him a lot. We're having this first communion class with his kid, Caroline, and he is there at every single session. I've never seen anything like it."

This is a different universe entirely from the excruciating non-recognition scenes with Joan, let alone those scorched-earth years as a child at Hyannis Port, where Joe and Rose so often dealt with the children — and each other — at arms' length, through personal secretaries and boarding school administrators. By 1996, caught by the cameras of C-Span gesticulating on the Senate floor or nose to nose with Larry King Live, a Ted Kennedy unavailable for decades was starting to reemerge. Across that broad yeoman face the features were back in place, restored to the old proportions. Kennedy's eyes had cleared, his color was healthy if florid, and Honey Fitz's solid jawline was again on view.

Congratulated on the weight he'd lost, Kennedy chuckled and credited it to Victoria's excellent Cajun cooking. "I thought since downsizing is in," he tossed off, "I'd better get on the treadmill. I wish I found the treadmill sooner." Not that the indulgences of a lifetime don't expire hard. Trapped on an elevator recently next to a man carrying a slice of pizza, Kennedy reportedly ventured "half-jokingly": . . . "You don't mind if I have a bite of that? I had a fruit salad lunch, and here it's not even 3:30, and I'm hungry."

———

Something profound was involved. When Kennedy had ventured in February of 1996 that "today's rising tide is lifting only some of the boats — primarily the yachts" he had in mind a good deal more than a variation on President Kennedy's dictum that "a rising tide lifts all boats." All along, for Ted, statements by his brother constituted writ. Now, though gently, what he was inferring was that Jack's economics were outmoded, the universe of postindustrial politics had shifted and it was up to *him* to interpret the working of the world. He'd become the lawgiver.

In somebody of Kennedy's deep-seated homage to his family this constituted a breakthrough. It was a very explicit signal that he was ready to bear the entire weight that came with taking himself seriously. Kennedy's life so far had amounted to stretches of hard work punctuated by evasions and high jinks whenever overwhelming responsibility threatened. Whatever price he'd paid, he'd unmistakably preferred that to failing at a series of roles he was not confident enough to fill.

He'd taken the long way around, building up his position and pushing out his range until even he himself could no longer evade the proportions of his accomplishment. It took the whirlwind of exposure that swept in once the Palm Beach incident broke, the anger and betrayal that even those closest to Kennedy showed openly, to make him understand that continuing to go through the motions of his dragged-out Reagan-era bachelor existence amounted to emotional self-immolation.

Unlike his brother the president, Edward Kennedy has proceeded all along on the immigrant's assumption that the game was rigged. He understood his calling as primarily to redeem the promises of the Constitution, to exploit the devices of parliamentarianism to return the system to balance.

Long before the phrase ever found its way into vogue, Kennedy had preoccupied himself with empowerment. Many of his sixties initiatives — to guarantee expanded franchise opportunities, to draft the gentry into the Viet Nam war — came out of his assumption that once more outsiders began to identify with government, social justice was certain to follow them in. Even what were derided at the time as Edward Kennedy's flirtations with the conservatives — the deregulation of buses and airlines, federal incarceration without parole of career criminals — came out of an abiding impulse to break up monopolistic interest groups, whether mobsters or airline executives. Let the system breathe.

The poor spooked Kennedy; they dogged his awareness like an unpaid bill. Perhaps more than anybody else in public life he felt their eyes, their expectations. Even as a child, before he volunteered his college hours helping out in settlement houses, Kennedy apprehended the meanness, the exasperation that ruined their lives. Again and again, confronted by the conditions in which millions of Americans subsisted, he would denounce the neglect and abuses he saw were commonplace. Such conditions were repellent, he would announce. They were *unacceptable* — a refrain over decades, echo of an older aristocracy.

As political generations turned, Kennedy depended with ever-increasing effect on his remarkable talent for evoking political decency among his colleagues, for reducing all argument to irresistible human elements. Slogans came and went — "You can't throw money at problems" was a Reaganite favorite — but in the end that made no sense, money was what you had, and day by day Kennedy held off the worst of the cuts. He hammered on education, and never gave up on health, and stalemated the predatory Right until the voters caught on.

Perhaps Kennedy fought so steadfastly over the years for the dispossessed and helpless because in the end he was one of them. Beneath the caustic ribbing and the hit-and-run roistering and all that unceasing competitiveness which disfigured the upbringing of the Kennedy brothers, each developed an isolation, an emotional disenfranchisement which kept them thrashing around quite wildly much of the time for gratification and support. Each of their wives had fought back differently. Joan was particularly subversive, first establishing her alcoholism, then blaming the weakness for her way of disappearing for days during a crisis, or badgering some family friend to sneak her a tumbler of ice and vodka at a party so Ted might think she was sipping water, or tugging down her panties to show her tan line to a security guard, or drifting in a diaphanous nightie through a political breakfast meeting at McLean.

Internally close to frantic with compounding responsibilities, intermittently wracked by loss, Kennedy jumped without apology on whatever relief presented itself. Inside, the loneliness grew year by year more oppressive. "When Teddy is after advice from somebody he trusts completely," one colleague as close as anybody to Kennedy once assured me, "he locks the door to his room and talks to himself."

These days he talks to Victoria. Their exchanges reportedly date from that first summer of 1991, when she had helped nerve him up to confess before the Kennedy School in October that he was finally able to "recognize my own shortcomings. . . . I alone am responsible for them, and I alone must confront them."

By Kennedy's lights, even this indirect mea culpa amounted to taking the pledge — "My name is Edward, and I've been incorrigible." While alcohol has always been a prickly subject around Kennedy, something he continually insisted he had no problem with, his efforts these days to confine himself to a quiet social highball probably approximates an admission of how often drink has unshackled the furies. Lifetime patterns are hard to expunge, and who can guess how easily a season of frustration and setbacks — or hubris — might uncork the bottle again? With Victoria rarely far from view, Kennedy's friends seem hopeful. "I'm writing a book here about death and redemption," I recently told one of them, "and I would not like to be surprised on publication day by Bad Teddy's resurrection."

He laughed, if warily. "I think you're OK," he assured me after a moment. "The bandages of Lazarus are long since gone."

Certain of the disfigurements these bandages were meant to conceal came through in our discussion in December. Kennedy started by musing about how it was that *health* turned into such a leitmotiv throughout his entire senatorial career. Touching on the litany of illness that had plagued his family, Kennedy seemed to drift without my leading him particularly into subjects more painful and searching by far than anything he'd ever been willing to talk to me about before. Buried resentments and anxieties came through in ways I couldn't have imagined in earlier years, when mention of the others invariably provoked a kind of kowtow toward all those Easter Island Heads. He could now confront, apparently, a great deal.

"Well, as a young child," Kennedy had begun, "I saw the way my older sister Rosemary had, you know, mental retardation. There was concern for her. But I also saw at that time what a loving and wonderful *person* she was, and how she was in so many ways, uh, almost gentler and tenderer and more loving even than other brothers and sisters. . . . I knew even as a younger person about the challenges that she faced. . . . And that probably made a subtle and not-so-subtle impression on me as a child who grew up in that family, and a consciousness just about some of the mysteries, you know, in terms of health care. . . ."

Rosemary. Of all the setbacks, her ordeal came earliest and somehow remained most poignant. She had, after all, lived on. Rose herself would call Rosemary's life "the first of the tragedies that were to befall us," and more was implied than that nature had crossed Rosemary's wires. The regret went very deep, beyond the stressful, competitive regimen that helped upset Rosemary, even beyond the botched prefrontal lobotomy behind the mother's back that left Rosemary to serve out the later decades of her long, angry life in St. Coletta's convent school in Jefferson, Wisconsin.

The question has arisen lately as to how limited Rosemary was, what role she found for herself inside that busy, ambition-ridden household. Rose Kennedy's personal assistant, Barbara Gibson, has published several fully coherent diary entries Rosemary wrote while traveling with her sister Eunice at twenty. Barbara Gibson herself concludes that, while apparently dyslexic, Rosemary was able to operate comfortably near the bottom of the normal range and that a procedure as radical as a lobotomy was in no way indicated. Family acquaintances who knew Rosemary as a child insist she was mildly retarded even then. Jack's Choate roommate, Lem Billings, would remember her in later adolescence as sexually frustrated and frantic at times, with an increasing tendency to lash out at all the clamor and competition around herself.

As Edward Kennedy underscores here, Rosemary was uniquely affectionate and understanding of the others. Barbara Gibson suggests that Rosemary's unexpected lobotomy, followed by her abrupt disappearance from the family circle, left the nine-year-old Teddy particularly confused and apprehensive, "never letting himself become too close to anyone, carrying anger, fear, and guilt trapped inside his troubled heart," frightened at some level that this could happen to him as well were he to disappoint the parents. Much of the concern — and a great deal of the family fortune — has gone into compensating successive generations of "very special children" for Rosemary's abiding anguish.

Kennedy got his introduction to another of the mysteries of health care when Jack came home from the Pacific in early 1944. "I remember my brother coming back when I was about twelve years old," Ted recalls, "the times when he was up in the hospital, and then recovering up in the Chelsea Naval Hospital and the difficulties that he had both from malaria and the wounds that he had. . . . I think that as a young person going into hospitals and seeing other people that were facing needs and suffering made a big impression on me. Obviously, with a brother that was so close. . . .

"As an older person I'd seen my brother's recovery in 1956. I spent a lot of time . . . my father used to let us go . . . we went down at Christmas and Easter to visit him down there [Palm Beach] but that was really the only time that we were expected to kinda come on home, because everybody was in school and college and working, but after my brother was sick he asked me if I couldn't come down and visit him on the weekends, so most of the weekends I'd come down and spend with him. You could see the impact of pain and suffering on him. . . ."

There again comes through Kennedy's sense of how *atom-ized* "that family" remained behind the walls of the estate, so unceasingly busy, such overpowering expectations. It seemed to wait for illness and death to wake them up momentarily. No wonder that health turned into the touchstone of Kennedy's career. That, fighting to protect others, he little by little contrived to heal himself.

Continuing down his list, Kennedy ticks off the death of his brother the president's infant son from Hyaline's Membrane

Disease. And his own son Teddy's battle with ligament cancer — "It was about $2,700 a treatment for three days every three weeks, and you needed it for two years. Fine, talk to parents whose children were going through similar experiences. They'd do it for five months, or six months, because that's all they could afford. And the burning impression about the fact that the difference between a child living and not living was whether you were able to afford the health insurance. . . ."

"I saw it again in my son Patrick, who is a chronic asthmatic, and still has about $2,500, $2,800 a year in terms of prescription drugs. . . ."

In Kennedy's mind, clearly, public policy derives not from noblesse oblige but rather simply extends out of his own life into the requirements of the community. His children got care; this year he'll mastermind efforts in the Senate to cover all children until they're eighteen. Whether pushing through funds to set up the Institute of Rehabilitation Medicine at the National Institute of Health, or cutting off insurance-industry attempts to game-plan the pool of policy-holders so that the premiums jump out of reach for people at serious risk, or threatening the HMOs with specific "rifle-shot" legislative remedies to deal with overnight birthing requirements or gag rules on doctors or drive-by mastectomies — all this in Kennedy's mind impacts, sooner or later, everybody. Family and Medical Leave? "I was always able to take three days off every three weeks when Teddy was so sick. I told Mike Mansfield I wouldn't be around every three weeks on a Friday. . . . I not only never risked losing my job, I was still getting paid while I was doing it. And Massachusetts would not have wanted me to be anyplace else." All politics remains personal.

———

Edward Kennedy could wind up serving longer than anybody so far in the history of the U.S. Senate. He's performed through good times as well as bad. Late in 1993, rummaging around the attic in McLean, Victoria Kennedy's son Curran came across a solicitation from the Green Bay Packers, circa 1956. "It read, 'Dear Mister Kennedy,'" Victoria laughs, "'you have been recommended for a professional football career. Our scouts have watched you and tell us you have promise.' My son was blown away. He adored Ted anyway, but that really clinched it. Ted tried to tell him it was a form letter, but Curran wasn't buying that. I finally said, 'Ted, you know, maybe the Green Bay Packers *could* use you. They're havin' a tough time too this season.' Isn't that hilarious?"

Maybe the Packers could. Kennedy is an established performer, and what he means to the country transcends issue or party. Dick Day, Alan Simpson's right hand man, probably catches it best: "Ted Kennedy is one of those guys who, when they have a list of the ten best senators and the ten worst senators around here, would very likely make both lists." It's a universal perception. At his staff party for Christmas of 1992, Kennedy appeared in horns and a mask while Victoria teased him. "Hello, beast," she opened. "You know you have been a beast at times."

What point in denying that? Beastliness reflects the bloodlines, that inspiration which years ago tempted Lewis Lapham to term Edward Kennedy a "Minotaur," a crossbreed of man and mythology, "a creature who carries within him all the 'opposed principles' that are the family legacy."

In Kennedy's family, and in the end in ours.

NOTES

EPIGRAPHS
v   "His brothers": Jack Beatty, *The Boston Globe,* July 30, 1994.
v   "When he": *The Boston Globe,* July 17, 1994.
v   "Below the belt": Henry Miller, *Stories, Essays, Travel Sketches,* (New York: M.J.F. Books, 1992), p. 77.

FOREWORD
viii   Daniel Webster had staying power: *Encyclopedia Britannica,* 1955 edition.

CHAPTER I
The background material for this chapter is from standard newspaper sources and private interviews, many off the record.
6   The day Ted finally: Aide to Senator Hart.
7   "This is quite a day on another front too!": J. Anthony Lucas, *Nightmare,* (New York: Viking, 1976), pp. 16, 17.
9   "Even more than Jack or Bobby": Saul Friedman, March 16, 1970.
11   Typical was a grilling: FAA hearings, March 16, 1970.

CHAPTER 2
12   "As your letter suggests": Edward Kennedy to Burton Hersh, January 29, 1971.
14   "When I came down here to work for Kennedy": Feinberg, September 1978.

15   "The ACLU performed": Parker, November 1979.

21   "The Senator would like to take you home tonight": Bo
      Burlingham, *Esquire,* November 19, 1975.

CHAPTER 3

24   "I don't have to kiss his ass": *The Boston Globe,* May 28, 1978.

25   Kennedy brooded all spring: *The New Republic,* April 29, 1978.

26   The President was guilty: *The Boston Globe,* July 29, 1978.

27   "We went down there just to fire a shot across the bow":
      Newsweek, December 5, 1978.

27   "special aura of appreciation": Ibid.

28   "He was a major player": Jan Kalicki, November, 1979.

29   "Whereas the United States": Cranston/Kennedy Joint
      Resolution on Taiwan, February 1, 1979.

29   "The President . . . asked me the other day": *The Boston Globe,*
      February 18, 1978.

30   With time and politics: Edward Kennedy speeches: Grinnell,
      Iowa, November 13, 1979; Manchester, N.H., November 21,
      1979.

CHAPTER 4

32   On May 2: *The Boston Globe,* May 3, 1979.

33   "various labor people were going around": John Durkin,
      November 1979.

34   "If I were to run, which I don't intend to": *Time Magazine,*
      June 25, 1979.

34   When Roosevelt was on the point: Richard Whalen, *The
      Founding Father,* (New York: Signet, 1966), p. 218.

35   "FDR . . . . sent Joe Kennedy to London": Ted Morgan, *F.D.R.,*
      (New York: Touchstone, 1985), p. 497.

35   To justify such repeated: Nigel Hamilton, *J.F.K.: Reckless Youth,*
      (New York: Random House, 1992), p. 368.

36   Jack himself: Whalen, op. cit., p. 440

36   Once Jack got elected: Ibid., p. 445.

36   Accused once: Jack Beatty, *The Boston Globe,* July 30, 1994.

39   By early spring: *The New York Times Magazine,* June 24, 1979.

40   Mudd set Kennedy up: quotes from broadcast itself, also *The
      Boston Globe,* October 31, November 6, 1979.

41   A Democratic National Committee straw poll: *The Boston Globe,* November 2, 7, 20, 1979.

42   "I look forward very very enthusiastically": *The Boston Globe,* November 8, 1979.

CHAPTER 5

44   "It was like, I want to be president": *The Boston Globe,* October 4, 1981.

45   "The Shah had the reins": *The Boston Globe,* December 3, 1979.

45   Shortly afterward Kennedy press spokesman: *The Boston Globe,* December 14, 1979.

45   "Ted Kennedy is the worst politician": Robert Shrum, December 16, 1993.

46   Kennedy's polls slipped: *The Boston Globe,* January 13, 1980.

46   "Kennedy had been drafted": Carey Parker, November 3, 1993.

47   Smith declined to designate: *The New York Times,* May 18, 1980.

47   "More than anything else Steve": Shrum, op. cit.

45   By April: *The Boston Globe,* May 6, 1980.

49   "a loud plaid suit": *The Boston Globe,* May 29, 1980.

50   If Ted *did* win: *The New York Times,* February 24, 1980.

50   "One of the side effects": *The Boston Globe,* April 19, 1980.

52   "We had no budget whatsoever": James Flug, November 29, 1993.

53   Kennedy's speech lifted: *The Boston Globe,* August 13, 1980.

CHAPTER 6

55   "Goddamn it": Shrum, op. cit.

56   "That's one thing about being leader": *The Boston Globe,* August 1, 1986.

56   On Labor and Human Resources: George Will, *The Boston Globe,* January 29, 1980.

56   "I know what you guys are thinking": Tom Rollins, December 1, 1993.

58   "After the '80 campaign": Edward Kennedy, December 2, 1993.

60   "tree ripe with the richest": *The Boston Globe,* July 17, August 14, September 25, 1981.

60   Aghast at the "jellybean economics": *The Boston Globe,* May 17, November 11, 1981.

61   "He doesn't steal credit": *Raleigh News and Observer,* November 17, 1987.

61   Kennedy was already criticizing: *The Boston Globe,* June 5, 1982.

61   "I've pulled Casey's nuts": Joseph Persico, *Casey,* (New York: Viking, 1990), pp. 373–75.

62   "you are a valuable member of the Committee": *The Boston Globe,* July 8, 1984.

63   "Instead of cutting off food stamps": *The Boston Globe,* June 28, 1982.

63   "Some people have even written": *The Boston Globe,* October 18, 1982.

63   "the decision that Joan and I have made": *The Boston Globe,* December 2, 1982.

64   "Jobs, a nuclear freeze": *The Boston Globe,* January 23, 1982.

64   "much increased my effectiveness": Edward Kennedy, December 2, 1993.

CHAPTER 7

66   "You know where he stands": *The Boston Globe,* November 16, 1984.

66   But Kennedy himself: Rick Atkinson, *The Washington Post Magazine,* April 29, 1990.

69   "C'mon Strom": Ibid.

69   Once Reagan was reelected: *The Boston Globe,* March 30, 1985.

69   "Congress is not only part of": *The Boston Globe,* October 11, 1985.

69   "You know, I liked you a lot": *The Boston Globe,* April 14, 1985.

70   "I admire him so much": *The Boston Globe,* February 20, 1982.

70   Nine of the eleven: *The New York Post,* January 5, 1987.

71   "When we took the Senate back": Rollins, op. cit.

71   "If you want to find Ted Kennedy": *The Washington Post Magazine,* April 29, 1990.

72   "compounded out of equal parts emotion": Dick Day, December 2, 1993.

72   "They had totally opposite senses of humor": Jerry Tinker, November 30, 1993.

73   "energetic, focused, and relentless": Jeff Blattner, November 29, 1993.

75   When Daniel Ortega came: Greg Craig, December 1, 1993.

76   "The feel-good invasion": *The Boston Globe,* January 24, 1990.

77   "I had always been somewhat reluctant": Edward Kennedy, December 2, 1993.

78   "My brothers had a relationship": Ibid.

79   Yet at the same time: *The Boston Globe,* March 28, 1990.

CHAPTER 8

81   "will murder you": Kelly, *GQ,* February 1990.

81   "You can talk to Ted": *The Boston Globe,* July 16, 1989.

82   "holds office but doesn't know what to do with it": *The Boston Globe,* March 7, 1989.

82   "major themes of the Clinton campaign": Nick Littlefield, November 30, 1993.

83   "Many of the liveliest stories": See heavy tabloid coverage. For example, *The National Enquirer,* April 14, 1992.

83   The news break in Damore's book: *The Boston Globe,* January 24, 1988.

84   "substantive, fortyish women": *Newsweek,* December 9, 1991, etc.

85   "I went out there thinking": Shrum, op. cit.

86   Ted Kennedy reportedly cut off John Culver: see Evan Thomas, *Newsweek,* December 9, 1991.

86   "you can bring anyone, or anything": Tinker, op. cit.

CHAPTER 9

89   "And we were visiting on the patio after dinner": *The Boston Globe,* December 7, 1991.

90   "many large parties": John Ney, *Palm Beach,* (Boston: Little Brown, 1966), p. 28.

91   "noticed both Patrick": *The Boston Globe,* December 7, 1991.

92   "was not the first night that week": John Aloysius Farrell, April 30, 1994.

92   "a Eurotrash kind of place": *The Boston Globe,* April 4, 1991.

92   Patrick — who overcame: *The Boston Globe,* December 10, 1991.

92   "What a comedown!": *The Concord Monitor,* July 27, 1988.

93   "He's my life": *The Boston Globe,* April 10, 1991.

93   "Patrick looked like he was having a terrible time": *The Boston Globe,* May 15, 1991.

94   "big families and scuba diving": *The Boston Globe,* April 7, 1991.

95   "Does your father embarrass you?" *The Boston Globe,* April 6, 1996.

95   "pulled out": *The Boston Globe,* May 15, 1991.

95   Originally Bowman ostensibly asserted: *The Boston Globe,* September 13, 17, 1991.

96   a number of objets d'art: *The Boston Globe,* April 17, May 11, 1991.

96   Nevertheless, the family did not waste time: *The Boston Globe,* April 3, 4, 1991.

97   "What I didn't anticipate": Farrell, op. cit.

98   "Kennedy stated that he was simply enjoying": *The Boston Globe,* April 9, 1991.

98   "The following July": reported in *The Boston Globe,* August 2, 3, 1991.

CHAPTER 10

100   "Palm Beach boozer": *Time Magazine,* April 29, 1991.

100   "the living symbol": *Newsweek,* December 9, 1991.

101   under another publisher: see *The Senator,* (New York, St. Martin's Press, 1992).

101   "have to be a little more attentive": *The Boston Globe,* June 9, 1991.

101   "disagreement with Ted": *The Boston Globe,* October 18, 1991.

101   "In my family and among my friends": *The Boston Globe,* October 7, 1993.

101 "I recognize my own shortcomings": *The Boston Globe,* October 26, 1991.

102 "Are we an old boys' club?": *The Boston Globe,* October 16, 1991.

102 "the vanishing views": *The Boston Globe,* September 13, 1991.

103 "In hindsight": Jeff Blattner, November 29, 1993.

104 "Even during the rape trial": David Nexon, November 30, 1993.

105 Victoria Reggie was frank: see background profiles in *The Boston Globe,* April 2, September 27, 1992; September 24, 1993. Also, *People Magazine,* March 30, 1992.

107 "She's smart": Peter Edelman, November 28, 1993.

107 "We saw each other": Victoria Kennedy, December 2, 1993.

108 Victoria usually cooked: *The Washington Post,* March 20, 1992.

109 With reelection in 1994 coming up: *The Boston Globe,* September 13, 28, 1993.

CHAPTER 11

110 "don't really have a relationship": *The Boston Globe,* December 8, 1992.

112 "invitation to drive the epidemic underground": *The Boston Globe,* September 22, 1987.

112 "Your private sector role": *The Boston Globe,* April 28, 1992.

112 "The senator decided early on": David Nexon, op. cit.

113 "tough, close decisions": *The Boston Globe,* June 16, 1993.

113 "Every effort to bring the American people together": *The Boston Globe,* June 20, 1993.

114 He worked a complicated: Pamela Barnes, *The Boston Globe,* September 9, 1993.

114 When Clinton returned to Boston: *The Boston Globe,* October 30, 1993.

115 "a shambles": see chapter 7, p. 70.

116 By then it hadn't gone unnoticed: *The Concord [N.H.] Monitor,* May 9, 1994.

116   A *Boston Globe* poll that spring: *The Boston Globe,* March 12, 1993.

117   "The fun goes out of it": *The Boston Globe,* August 3, 1986.

117   the Senator cranked a window down: Paul Donovan, November 30, 1993.

118   By October of 1993: *The Boston Globe,* October 6, 1993.

CHAPTER 12

119   only 38 percent felt that he merited: *The Boston Globe,* May 14, 1994.

120   "My God, what weather!": Edward Kennedy, June 20, 1994.

124   "strategy has always been to raise plenty of money early": Milton Gwirtzman, April 1, 1994.

124   "If people believe the answer": *The Boston Globe,* June 22, 1994.

CHAPTER 13

Many of the details and statistical material throughout this election were gathered by the outstanding political reporters of *The Boston Globe.* In general, only major features or controversial details will be attributed.

126   "learn-fare": *The Boston Globe,* June 17, 1994.

127   "One of my two potential opponents": *The Boston Globe,* June 18, 1994.

127   In early July: *The Boston Globe,* July 3, 1994.

127   "looked good, spoke well": *The Boston Globe,* July 12, 1994.

127   "full flounder": *The Boston Globe,* July 23, 24, 1994.

128   "The Old Lion": *The Boston Globe,* June 8, 14, 1994.

130   "Many companies now have wellness programs": Edward Kennedy, op. cit.

131   "I'm sure there have been a lot of things": *The Boston Globe,* June 3, 1996.

131   not to mention the $150,000: *The Boston Globe,* October 11, 1994.

132   "Teddy, you do it": *The Boston Globe,* May 24, 1996.

132   "This has been a tragedy": *The Boston Globe,* July 19, 1996.

132   "just an old career pol": *The Boston Globe,* June 2, 1994.

132   retain Monroe Inker: *The Boston Globe,* September 9, 1994.

132   a reputable poll: *The Boston Globe,* September 17, 1994.

133 the campaign's fire-eating press aide: *The Boston Globe,* September 21, 1994.

133 "not an issue, and it shouldn't be": *The Boston Globe,* May 22, 1994.

133 Orlando de Sola: *The Boston Globe,* August 8, 1994.

134 This subject he refused to discuss: *The Boston Globe,* September 7, 1994.

134 A local Catholic spokesman: Ibid.

135 "perverse and reprehensible": *The Boston Globe,* July 15, August 7, 1994.

135 Near the end of August: *The Boston Globe,* August 26, 1994.

135 "$50 million dollar fund": *The Boston Globe,* June 18, 1994.

135 "He will intentionally try": *The Boston Globe,* September 28, 1994.

136 "We got together and we changed": Robert Shrum, March 27, 1996.

137 "I mean, the balanced budget amendment": *The Boston Globe,* July 7, 1994.

137 Sally Jacobs was trailing Kennedy: *The Boston Globe,* June 2, 1994.

138 "I feel you might, ah": Edward Kennedy, op. cit.

138 "Vicki agrees with me": Edward Kennedy letter to B.H., July 6, 1994.

139 As advertising bills piled up: *The Boston Globe,* October 22, 1994.

139 Kennedy's lawyers now reached: *The Boston Globe,* September 29, November 10, 1994.

139 "multiple-choice": *The Boston Globe,* September 22, 1994.

140 Here was a man: *The Boston Globe,* October 20, 1994.

140 "just another robber baron": *The Boston Globe,* September 23, 1994.

141 In July: *The Boston Globe,* September 30, 1994.

142 "We'd run the spots": Shrum, op. cit.

142 "I'd love to help": *The Boston Globe,* October 10, 1994.

142 a remote investment of the Joseph P. Kennedy enterprises: *The Boston Globe,* October 24, 25, 1994.

143 "patently ridiculous": *The Boston Globe,* October 29, 1994.

143 Kennedy's willingness during the previous year: *The Boston*

Globe, November 4, 1994.

143 "flip-flop-flip. . . .": *The Boston Globe,* October 21, 1994.

CHAPTER 14

144 "a tongue-tied blowzy": *The Boston Globe,* October 31, 1994.

145 "The entire national press corps": Shrum, op. cit.

145 "why is this race even close": Most of this debate material came from the videotapes of the two debates.

148 Within hours of the Tuesday debate: *The Boston Globe,* October 26, 1994.

152 "Mr. Romney," Kennedy himself announced: *The Boston Globe,* October 31, 1994.

CHAPTER 15

153 "I think it was a surprise": Carey Parker, March 26, 1996.

155 "I remember one meeting in 1980": Shrum, op. cit.

159 Kennedy's payroll currently numbers fifty-eight: Lloyd Grove, *The Washington Post,* July 9, 1996.

159 "it seemed like virtually the consistent figure": Adam Clymer, *The New York Times,* August 11, 1996.

159 "I don't think Senator Kennedy has *ever*": Nick Littlefield, March 26, 1996.

160 He put together a quorum: *The Boston Globe,* May 14, 1995.

161 "built around lavish tax cuts that primarily benefit the wealthy": *The Boston Globe,* July 5, 1995.

163 "That's in the briefing sheet": *The Washington Post,* op. cit.

163 The effort was afoot: *The Boston Globe,* September 21, 1995.

164 "This is one cookie jar": *The Boston Globe,* October 28, 1995.

164 By April of 1996 eight: *The Boston Globe,* April 26, 1996.

165 Two days before he died: *The Boston Globe,* October 18, 1995.

165 "socialized medicine by the back door": *The Boston Globe,* April 20, 1996.

165 "For him to pick up the pieces like that": John Aloysius Farrell, March 26, 1996.

CHAPTER 16

168 Six weeks later: *The Boston Globe,* April 28, 30, 1996; May 6, 1996.

169   Richard Viguerie: *The Boston Globe,* April 26, 1996.

170   "carrying her own clubs": *The Boston Globe,* January 23, 1995.

171   the shy and rather reflective Patrick: Most of the material here comes from Joshua Seftel's 1996 cinema vérité film *Taking On the Kennedys.*

171   he developed a reputation for persistence and integrity: *The Boston Globe,* June 19, 1995.

173   "a work horse, not a show horse": *The Boston Globe,* November 10, 1994.

173   more conservatively on social issues: *The Boston Globe,* June 19, 1995.

173   By then Kennedy's delaying tactics with the health bill: *The New York Times,* August 4, 1996.

175   Kennedy allies like Steve Early: *The Boston Globe,* November 21, 1994.

177   "They don't want to do it because they are basically": *The Boston Globe,* July 9, 1996, part of a three-part series on corporate welfare.

179   Congress remained trapped in partisan deadlock: *The Boston Globe,* May 19, 1996.

180   He shamed the majority: *The Washington Post,* op. cit.

CHAPTER 17

186   "I thought since downsizing is in": *The Boston Globe,* May 11, 1996.

186   Trapped on an elevator recently: *The Washington Post,* op. cit.

191   Rose herself would call Rosemary's life "the first": Nigel Hamilton, *J.F.K.,* p. 412.

191   Rose Kennedy's personal assistant: Barbara Gibson, *Rose Kennedy and Her Family,* (New York: Birch Lane Press, 1995), p. 62.

191   Jack's Choate roommate, Lem Billings: Hamilton, op. cit., p. 411.

191   Barbara Gibson suggests that: Gibson, op. cit., p. 73.

194   "It read, 'Dear Mr. Kennedy,' ": Victoria Kennedy, op. cit.

194   Dick Day: Dick Day, op. cit.

ACKNOWLEDGMENTS

Before mentioning anyone else, I suppose, it is important to acknowledge my debt to my subject, Senator Edward M. Kennedy. Our acquaintanceship goes back a good part of both our lives — Kennedy's years at Harvard overlapped my own, and I knew who he was even then — but I did not get interested in his progress as a politician until the latter nineteen-sixties, when I attempted the first of what would turn into periodic attempts to characterize him, at that point for the editors of *Esquire* in 1967. Once the article appeared, word got back, Kennedy was not pleased. He was already accustomed to the euphoric picture-and-text glorification of himself and his photogenic young family, most often out sailing, that the glossier magazines of the period kept providing; although my piece was in large part admiring, Kennedy was already sensitive enough about his image not to have discovered too many unexpected qualifications floating up through the prose, too many contrary ripples. He pulled back.

By then I had started a full-length biography of the senator, *The Education of Edward Kennedy* (Morrow, 1972). I had an access problem for awhile. Then the Chappaquiddick episode blew up his life; my treatment looked better in retrospect; Kennedy gave me as much of his own time and involvement with his staff as I could possibly use.

In 1979 I accepted an assignment from *The Washingtonian* for a lead article on Kennedy on the eve of his 1980 campaign for the Democratic nomination, several of the highpoints of which I've included here. Relations remained very cordial until the piece actually appeared. Then, throughout the eighties, when I was much in the District, I made a point of stopping by Kennedy's office. Without exception he made some time for me.

Over that struggling decade I got to know Kennedy better, invariably gracious and welcoming without the threat any forthcoming piece of writing clearly poses in his mind. He remained in many ways quite shy — even uncertain — underneath, frequently dealing with the stresses of the world through his sly, rueful, rather delicate sense of humor. He saw too much very often, and reflected this behind closed doors by exercising his extraordinary talent for accents and mimicry. Everything that he glimpsed helped fortify his act.

In 1994, weakened by the Palm Beach scandal over Willy Smith's alleged rape, Kennedy faced a serious Republican challenge for reelection. I agreed to do another piece for *Esquire,* which I have borrowed from here to present his state of mind at the time. Again, Kennedy gave me plenty of access. Again, when the article came out, despite the outside consensus that the article in large terms presented Kennedy and his enterprise as substantial, valuable, Kennedy — and reportedly his influential younger wife, Victoria — felt miffed, underappreciated, overinspected.

In 1996 Steerforth Press approached me with the possibility of resurrecting the biographical essay, a very personalized treatment of Kennedy and his political importance. Kennedy's office remained ambivalent about the project. He himself was overscheduled. He had his own memoirs in mind now, and preferred to keep his impressions to himself. Typically, Kennedy did authorize his senior aides to give me whatever I wanted, so substantively I had more than enough to round my portrait off. Then, just as the book was slipping into production, Kennedy's office came through with an eleventh-hour reprieve, word that the senator was available for a brief final interview, a survey of political prospects as the millennium ended. This was heartening news. It meant that, beyond the dust bowl of imminent publication, the senator and I will presumably be able to resume as before.

Whatever the senator's reservations, at no time has he ever cut me off from fraternization with either his immediate staff people or that rather amorphous entourage of his friends and colleagues and supporters and one-time employees who together comprise a kind of unofficial government-in-exile. There are now four or five generations of staff who have moved on to their lives after years of serving the senator. Some have become wealthy, authentic dignitaries in their own right; others have largely dropped from sight; one or two have been lucky to escape the penitentiary. I've stayed in touch with quite a number, who have regularly kept me abreast of the ins and outs of Kennedy's progress. In this book, I've tended to leave them out of the source notes, generally at their own request. Scholars in the field might want to consult the back matter of *The Education*.

I remain especially grateful to the surviving staff people in Kennedy's offices while I was researching this book, and mention them here in alphabetical order: Jeffrey Blattner, Paul Donovan, Pamela Hughes, Victoria Kennedy (consulting), Nick Littlefield, Melody Miller, David Nexon, Carey Parker, Robert

Shrum (consulting), the late Jerry Tinker. Special thanks to Dick Day, Peter Edelman, Jim Flug, Greg Craig, Milton Gwirtzman, and Tom Rollins. Jack Farrell of *The Boston Globe* deserves a line of his own.

For help and support over the years I want to thank the editors from successive regimes at *Esquire:* the late Harold Hayes and Don Erikson from the early days, and Jamie Malanowski more recently. Jack Limpert of *The Washingtonian* proved sympathetic and savvy while Kennedy was pondering his presidential run. At Steerforth the strongminded and astute Thomas Powers has prodded most effectively. And naturally a plug for my literary agent, Jonathan Matson, whose knack for coordinating this sort of project is certainly in a class by itself.

On the composition end of things, in Bradford, New Hampshire, I again have to thank the all but imperturbable Janet Byfield, whom I am aware I regularly put to the test. And of course, as ever, my loyal and durable wife, Ellen.

Burton Hersh
Bradford, New Hampshire
May, 1997

INDEX

A NOTE ON THE AUTHOR

BURTON HERSH is a veteran writer on American politics and the author of *The Education of Edward Kennedy* (1972), still the standard treatment of the Senator's early career. Hersh's most recent book is *The Old Boys: The American Elite and the Origins of the CIA.* He lives in Bradford, New Hampshire and St. Petersburg, Florida.

A NOTE ON THE BOOK

This book was composed by Steerforth Press using a digital version of Bembo, a typeface produced by Monotype in 1929 and based on the designs of Francesco Griffo, Venice, 1499. The book was printed on acid free papers and bound by Quebecor Printing ~ Book Press Inc. of North Brattleboro, Vermont.